I0084950

Little Squares with Colors

A Different way to look at Autism

Christina Dagnelli

Crusty Productions

CRUSTY

PRODUCTIONS

Little Squares with Colors: A Different way to Look at Autism

Crusty Productions
PO Box 22
Maple Shade, NJ 08052

This book is an original publication of Crusty Productions

The names and identifying characteristics of some of the people and places mentioned have been changed.

Neither the publisher nor the author is engaged in rendering professional advice or services to the reader. Suggestions are not intended as a substitute for consulting your physician. Neither the author or publish shall be liable or responsible for any loss injury or damage resulting from the readers use or imitation of any information or suggestions in this book.

Copyright 2010 Christina Dagnelli
Cover design provided by Create a Space & Christina Dagnelli
Edited by Keith Souders
All rights reserved

No part of this book may be reproduced, scanned, distributed or printed without written consent of the publisher.

ISBN 978-0-9842472-19 Trade Soft cover

First Edition

For Noah and all those who love someone on the Autism Spectrum

Acknowledgements

I would like to thank everyone that has supported me during the time I decided to write this book. I am grateful to have my cheerleaders Carolyn, Vikki, and Heather all who have been very excited and enthusiastic about this project. And my technical helpers Keith, Kevin, and Joe who have helped with editing, design; and taking care of my hair, my dogs, and my sanity sometimes. I mostly need to thank Noah for being the inspiration and the challenge that he is. This book truly has given me momentum to complete the work on other projects that I have been working on for many years. I have learned much during this process and now I know I can do it.

CHAPTERS

Introduction

I was an inquisitive child, and my parents and grandparents would respond to one of my numerous questions with, "What are you writing a book?" Sometimes I would have a smart-ass comeback and say that I was, which they would reply, "Well leave that chapter out and make it a mystery." Their words of encouragement have led me here writing this book only it's about my son Noah and his Autism. I do not need to leave any chapters out to make this book a mystery; whether you know a lot or a little about Autism, one thing is certain; it is a mystery.

I am not one who believes all things happen for a reason; however I do believe we can find reason in all things that happen. This is almost the same thing. Many people have made this statement to us along our journey, and I am sure it is their intention to be comforting. But I figure, finding the reason is a personal choice. I don't think Noah's Autism was a premeditated or determined plan and that his pain exists for us to be better people, for that is a self-centered way to think.

Little Squares with Colors

I am introspective, a thinker by nature, I like to pick things apart and examine them. I find what motivates people and what doesn't motivate them interesting. So it is more natural for me to find my own reason in what happens or doesn't happen to me if I choose to find it to begin with. Regardless of how enlightened I may have been before there was Noah, regardless of what I learned during this time, life is all about that. You will always learn new things, and put forth and apply the things you have learned.

Autism is a lot of fun it is a life of unpredictability. So at least you are never bored, just exhausted. And it has ebbed and flowed like all tides do, and has changed its complexion a bit. Certain things improve while new things pop up that may be more difficult. This is no different than any other part of life; it's just unfortunate when it is tied to your child. In simple terms though, it's like being stuck in the terrible twos for extra years, without all the fluffy cute kid stuff.

I also cannot predict whom I am dealing with. Some days Noah is even tempered, and it's just maybe two or three times as much work as it should be. The rest of the time it's a big cluster of bombardment, constant noise and chatter, mostly to himself, and never about anything. He likes to hear himself talk for different reasons than others do, but it is just as annoying after you deal with it all day every day. There is also all the repeating that you have to do. Repeating questions he didn't hear the first five times, repeating instructions for the hundredth time, repeating the same rules about where food goes, or trash; or how to wash his hands, how to clean up. Stop pulling the dog's head, or the cat's fur; you can't pick up a cat by its side fur. No the dogs don't like their tails pulled, or their feet either. Thankfully he has not yet noticed their private parts. Repeating yourself repeating yourself. Not to mention there is always a lot of cleaning up, since that is not his forte. Competing backgrounds, which is a technical term for when there are a bunch of items in one area, such as toys on the floor; causes him stress and anxiety because he can't find things.

There is also all the stepping on you; random scratching, hitting you in the face or other assorted potentially injurious behavior, because he doesn't notice you, or he thinks it's funny, or he is having a meltdown. But the biggest challenge is the world exists only in his mind.

If you feel tired, sick, or hungry, and you say: "I have to throw up. I need to go to the bathroom." You would think at least after you said this the second or third time he would let you out of his room, but No.

And he's fast, so picking him up and moving him doesn't work unless I am okay with getting my own fingers slammed in the bedroom door. However, I can see this may be a better option than throwing up all over the place, since I would have to clean that up afterwards.

Then there is the constant feeding schedule. He does not sense his hunger well, but you will know too much time has passed when he is suddenly beating the crap out of you because the banana you gave him was broken in half. Sometimes it is the opposite; he is in touch with his hunger because he is asking for something every fifteen minutes. Try getting laundry done, making a phone call, writing an email, looking up the weather, or work from home, when you know if you are not just staring at him the whole time, you will likely be cleaning up, marker off the walls, water from the bathroom floor, paint off the dogs, or if you are very lucky and going to the bathroom. He may call 911 just because Curious George and Elmo do. Of course I have also learned not to go outside without keys since he could lock me out making me climb in a tiny window and bruise myself so bad it temporarily affects how I walk, but I have also learned no one else will ever want to break into my house either.

A lot of these things are the same when you are home with a young child, but the difference is the intensity and the fact it continues on despite consequences, despite following through, and despite time.

I understand it is harder to be him than it is to be me, I still don't like my stuff ruined, to be beat on, have my pets hurt, or to be bombarded with all the excessive noise, requests and explanations. It has given me perspective on what it's like to be him.

So I manage as best as possible with hot showers, music and singing. Of course this has to be when he is not around. I still sing in the car whenever I can go out in it by myself, I sometimes just drive around the streets near my house when I am on my way back from some errand, just to have a few extra minutes. I survive it because I do not think about the frustrations most of the time, and just get through the day as best as possible. I let those thoughts cross my mind, only when I am on the other side of my mind with those thoughts (typically 3 months into winter), is when I get overwhelmed and sad. Music helps, I have several songs that help get me through. *Show Must Go on*, by Queen is a favorite because it speaks about persevering through moments. How we feel on the inside is often temporary and to not get stuck in that place but rather push through. Sometimes if you don't feel brave, it is best to fake it until you actually do feel brave, because you will from doing the things that brave people do.

I wrote this book for two reasons. The selfish reason of needing to put all that has happened and is happening in a place, to compartmentalize it. I also wrote this for the same reason most people would share something of this nature, because when you go through something and learn from it, you want to help those still there, just starting out, because it is your duty to do so. And since I have been the documenter of all things for most if not all of my life, writing a book is just what I had to do. I hope that this not only helps those in the situation but it also enlightens their support system.

Autism rate statistics are stated to be 1 in 150 in 2009. And there are many people who know someone or are someone on the spectrum. Disorders like Tourettes syndrome, Dyslexia, Obsessive Compulsive Disorder, Attention Deficit disorder and anxiety are all parts of Autism. Repetition of sounds or actions that are part of Tourettes and OCD are part of Autism, as are personality issues with Dyslexia and Anxiety. They are just labels to make it easier to describe without having to list all of the attributes of the situation.

So many of us know people that have these disorders, whether they are diagnosed or not. Maybe your uncle who only orders chicken parmesan when he goes out to eat is possibly on the spectrum, or he really really likes it. Perhaps someone you know that just drives you crazy, or is difficult in some way is because of a disorder they do not know they have or they haven't bothered to tell you about. It doesn't excuse them, but it should help you understand what does not come naturally. Ultimately it is up to them to make their own choices and sometimes correct themselves.

You may even realize that you yourself share some of these issues, perhaps you have to have certain order in your home, or you are easily distracted, or you can't understand why people don't understand you. Or if you're like me, you can't stand certain sounds, and sometimes when you talk people need to be air traffic controllers because you change the subject so many times, but that is how your mind works.

Despite my tendency to ramble on, I did my best to keep this book on the shorter side, since many of us parents have limited time to read.

This is our story.

ACT ONE

Welcome to the Show
Please come inside

"You can't have too many friends, but you can have too many enemies."

Noah age 11

Chapter One - Show Must Go On

"I'll Face it with a grin, I'm never giving in, on with the show." ~ Queen

I was never certain whether I wanted to be married and have children, or not. I never imagined what my wedding day would be like, but did think about what kind of groom I would want. I would change my mind many times on whether I would want this or just be content with living with a bunch of animals somewhere in California or Hawaii.

When I was in my early 20s my gynecologist informed me I likely had endometriosis or fibroids based on the problems I had monthly, and informed me if I ever wanted to have a baby, I better do it by the time I was twenty-four or it may never happen. No pressure or anything, and being in your early twenties are overwhelming enough, now there is a clock ticking. So the previous dance of do I want to be married with children or not still continued until I was about twenty-six, when I just decided I didn't care either way anymore. This gave me relief, and a year later I was committed to a longtime friend, and shortly thereafter I was pregnant.

Surprisingly my female organs were still functioning three years past their deadline. This was my final test on the lesson of worry, for had I known years before this would happen; I wouldn't have wasted so much energy on any of it. Goes to show how wasteful worry is-you can't get that time back you spent worrying about something that never happens. (Unless you have a time machine.). You also can't get the time back you spent worrying about something that does eventually happen. Why not enjoy the road beforehand things can always change. I hope to sink this lesson into Noah's head, if even just a little.

I never imagined, either, what my child would be like. Besides that, if I did have a girl, I looked forward to playing with Barbie's again, but did not look forward to the years when little girls are becoming little women and are treating themselves like Barbie. I did hope that the curse my mother put on me, you know the one your parents give you when you're challenging them. "I hope one day you have a child just like you!" I hoped it would come to fruition and my child would be just like me, since my mother never knew how good she had it. But I had a boy instead, and Noah may look a lot like me; we are as different as peas and carrots, but at least they go well together.

I felt ready to be a parent though, feeling balanced within myself, having overcome many of my own obstacles in life. I like many have survived a troubled childhood with an alcoholic parent and the eventual divorce of my parents. My dad remarrying and having to adjust to this new life, and eventually losing them when times became ridiculous, full of stress, and a lack of understanding. My sister who has dyslexia had numerous struggles, my parents didn't understand (they had us young and in their 20's). There were times she ran away, she was my responsibility, and I had to put college on hold to make sure she made it to school, because no one helped my Dad when he split with his second wife. My sister and I also had to deal with our mother's murder when she was 15 and I was 19. I didn't escape the heart break department either with losing a dear friend, who also was my first love, when we were far too young to lose anyone. And then there is my second love who turned out to be gay. Though that can and will fill another book, it was also a victory, for no longer did I feel inadequate. And it motivated me to fully accept myself, which I believe is the key to finding your own happiness.

We all have our sad stories, and our struggles, it's what we do with them that matters. When you can do better, you do better.

Somehow I managed to stay off drugs and mostly sane. I felt I had a lot to offer a child, many things I learned -

how I loved school, how important friends are and how mine became my close family that I just wasn't blessed with. I was ready to handle the potential strife of childhood, how to overcome low self-confidence and how to be your own star. I was ready thanks to Bill and Claire Huxtable, and the parents from *Family ties* and *Growing Pains*, and mostly from much time spent contemplating the universe and everyone's place in it. I knew I would be good at it and it would be challenging but fun. I knew it would be better than my previous job in Transportation with the betrayals of the corporate world, despite that job's family like atmosphere, but again, that is another book.

With all that I did know, I didn't know my first and only child would have Autism. I didn't know much about Autism except from my cousin Ray who was always just Ray and "slow" to us. He in fact never got an official diagnosis until he was in his late 20s and was diagnosed with Aspergers Syndrome, a syndrome I will become familiar with; because it is where my Childs diagnosis is supposed to eventually lead. So if I had to look at Ray as the future, I was at least comfortable in that I have known him all his life. But I also knew all of the struggles he had fitting in, and how lonely he was at times. I also remember the echoes of childhood of him repeating himself a lot, and having a real talent and interest in video games.

"Colecio! Colecio!" Raymond would excitedly ask for at any of our family get-togethers at my house. I also remembered how well his sister Helen took care of him and how she also got him to do embarrassing things that he would do even if he were objecting.

"Raymond come on pull your pants down, moon us!" Helen would request laughingly

"Oh alright" Raymond would say in a protesting manner but do it anyway.

But overall she was a mini-therapist to him, making him talk and ask for things, being his playmate. Of course we didn't know that at the time, and only many years later did we realize this. If not for her, who knows if Raymond would've ever really talked. He didn't say much of anything the first five years of his life. In the back of my mind I must have remembered all this, and was partially why I knew something was off with Noah.

Fortunately for both Noah and myself, I am a bit of an animated person; I live by the saying "live laugh and love often" and the motto of "seize the day". I enjoy drinking in life whenever I can. I was also voted most talkative in high school for all 3 *"Who's Who"* in 7th, 8th and 12th grades. Yes, I am undefeated, and that annoying quality has turned out to be a method of therapy and saving grace that has kept Noah from the pit of autism. It isn't a cure in itself, but I know it has kept him from being further impaired, since I was naturally applying therapy the entire time from my chatty mouth.

So as it turns out there was a good reason for my talkativeness after all! I still wouldn't say it was "The Plan" as there are many chatterboxes out there with chatterbox children, and there are many parents of kids with Autism and on the spectrum that are not as animated. Maybe I don't have a reason because I don't need one.

Noah spent many years not being able to talk to me. It is poetic in an ironic way. I just wasn't willing to leave it that way and leave those barriers intact. I chose to let my mouth be a battering ram, to break through, even if it only happened for just a few moments here and there.

Why this has happened isn't important - what we learn from this experience is what matters. I believe Autism also teaches us to be more tolerant, more patient and never to give up hope. And if there is any kind of lesson, perhaps it is for other people not even directly involved. There is an enormous amount of patience required when dealing with behavioral issues in anyone. Sometimes we get impatient waiting for the other person to do what we ask or stop acting in a certain way that is causing us discomfort, we forget what we may be asking of them. How maybe what we want is hard for them to do in a way we don't understand because it falls into what we do naturally. Coming home from work or school is just that to most of us, but for other people, it is a big transition, a change in smells, sights and sounds. It is different expectations, different things happen, and there is nothing natural about it to them. So we take for granted our own functionality because it is natural to us. We all know people that take their own life for granted. My own seize-the-day attitude and desire to live in the moment is the opposite of Noah's who is always thinking about the next moment and generally is anxious in the moment.

I would like him to learn to stop and smell the roses. Whether or not it is necessary for happiness, I just believe it is hard to be happy if you never slow down to actually feel it. There are so many great things children can influence and shape in their parents' lives, Being in this situation creates more gratitude when times are not full of stress. And stress for Noah is always there under the surface; anxiety is part of Autism and it is always present, like a pot of boiling water. It only rears its head when it is left on the stove for too long.

June 2002 Darkness Creeps in Like a Thief

Poor kid can't even lay flat in his bassinette, and I think of what trouble I went through to get the dang thing, and even how annoyed I made the person who actually bought this for us. Noah has not slept more than maybe one or two nights in it. Every time you lay him down in it, he would have that startle reflex as if he didn't know where he was. At the time I didn't know that was not supposed to happen.

Noah has been sleeping every night in his car seat, semi propped up next to my side of the bed, all snuggled up. This he seems to find comfortable; the bassinette seemed to really stress him out and since he is so little and can't' talk, figure we should listen to him. I first thought maybe it was acid reflux, maybe something I ate is not agreeing with him, though, I never heard of a baby getting acid reflux, or heartburn every night. I have a varied diet, so I could not imagine what it was. But why else would he have to sleep like that?

This went on until he was too big for the car seat and fell out of it one night, and then we moved him to his crib. The crib was okay he seemed much better than he was for the past six months or so. Part of me was still wondering why he was having this problem, was it because of the Hydrocele?

A Hydrocele if you don't know (Which I didn't) is a fluid filled sac surrounding the testicle caused by a tube that normally closes off while in utereo. It can heal on its own, but in Noah's case it did not. It was fixed with surgery when he was 1 years-old to prevent a hernia from occurring from his intestines getting caught in it. During the trauma of childbirth, one of his testicles was twisted which is likely what caused it. It was a sketchy delivery.

I did not have the easiest of pregnancies nor was it the worst possible scenario either. I had read about many horror stories of being bed ridden for more than half of the time in a hospital, which though I enjoyed my stay in, would of gotten old if I was there for months on end. I did however develop high blood pressure, something I'd never had a problem with, and in fact I had been previously treated for the opposite problem. I did have to curb all of my normal activities and was put on mandatory bed rest, with an extra 1 hour nap a day. This was very confining and not like my normal existence.

Latent, or early, labor had begun around Mother's Day, which I believe was about two weeks before the delivery happened. So I was very lucky to be walking around dilated three centimeters for all that time, it was terrific. If labor had not begun on its own Induction would have occurred on Thursday May 30th

Labor finally progressed on May 27th at 5 pm with definite contractions by 3 am I could not sleep and just wanted to go to the hospital, for the hope of being able to sleep. Little did I know I would be awake until 10pm the next day. When I got there I was dilated to 5 cm and I was told if this did not progress by 7 am I was being sent home. No way was that going to happen so I willed it by walking. They did admit me.

Several hours later, still in pain and still no baby the doctors suggested the epidural. Which I was not going to get originally, because I was deluded I guess, but after being in constant pain for almost 24 hours and also having endured 2 weeks of early labor I graciously accepted it. I later found out the reason it was so painful was because Noah was "sunny side up" facing the wrong way and causing something called back labor. If schools really want to curb teenage pregnancy they should really teach you about this, for I had never heard of it until this moment. Soon after the needle I was given Pitocin, which is a drug used to increase contractions, it was used hoping it would increase dilatation. They also decided to break my water, since it wasn't happening on its own.

At this point they discovered the baby had passed his first stool or Meconium. Good thing I had read about that before this otherwise I would have had some crazy ideas on what it was. And in some offbeat way he had begun pooping on me right from the beginning. But because of this it gave me a slight fever and the baby an elevated heart rate. By 6pm dilation reach nine centimeters; if it did not progress by 7pm I was going to have an emergency C-section, which I was definitely not happy about. I burst into tears like a baby myself. This now has become the furthest from a natural delivery as possible, and having had surgery in the past and not reacting well to the drugs, I was frightened.

They had to do what they felt was right because of the dang poop. Surgery proceeded normally with some extra bleeding although closing did take a little longer than usual. What I remember most was their commenting on how big the baby was. He was nearly nine pounds; I am just over five feet tall, and was a small under six pound baby myself. So the need for a C-section started to make more sense. I was awake but not with it, I had a boy apparently. Not the great bringing into the world I had hoped, but he came out mostly ok with Apgar scores of nine and nine.

There were some small problems revealed right away, he had a twisted scrotum and later discovery of the hydrocele Which if it doesn't close naturally the child can get a hernia.

Noah spent his first two hours or so in the Neo-natal Intensive Care Unit for difficulty in breathing (rapid breath) to expel fluids from the final stages of labor. And he spent every evening in the nursery and probably a lot more time there than I would have liked or expected.

I was planning on breast-feeding; from all the reading I did while pregnant it sounded like the healthiest option. The baby would get vital immunity, there is special bonding time involved, it costs less and was more convenient, and Mom as a bonus gets to be a calorie-burning machine. The last part is not true; at least it wasn't for me. To this day I still have 15-20 pounds left over from this pregnancy despite an active lifestyle, good eating habits and regular exercise. But whatever, least of the problems around here are whether or not I can wear my old jeans, which I never really liked anyway.

When it came time to feed Noah for the first time, it was a problem; he couldn't latch on and would just cry and get all red in the face over it. The hospital had lactation consultants who were regularly coming in and out of my room to help. I would say despite having three different consultants with many years of training between them, Noah never latched on for more than three minutes, if that. They did provide an electric pump to keep the milk stimulated and flowing; I had already bought a hand pump (just because I am an over achiever like that) and figured I would make additional milk. Little did I know it would be my only way of feeding him breast milk.

I was pumping with the manual pump at home to keep up my supply and to feed him while we were still trying to feed at the breast. However, I began to lose hope, and with every meal came anxiety and frustration, so I started to hate it. I was so angry that I was not able to Breastfeed him. I blamed my body and the C-section and felt my body let me down. Then I decided that I could feed him the way I wanted and had been all along. I made the conscious decision to stop trying to feed him at the breast, and just concentrate on expressing every bottle, and hopefully be able to do this for as long as possible.

I admit it was no picnic; in the beginning it was so time consuming and boring. I had to pump eight to ten times a day to mimic what he would have been doing himself. I followed a schedule but fed him as he requested it. I was never sure how long I would be able to keep this regimen up; each pumping session took fifteen to twenty minutes and each feeding about the same. Do the math; he ate approximately ten to twelve times a day because he could only handle two ounces or so at a time (when I pumped I usually got twice the amount.) So on average it was like feeding him twenty times a day, which comes to about eight hours of feeding time. For the first time in my life, I took it one day at a time. Giving myself small goals: first try to survive the first six weeks, then try to get to three months (which would be a milestone concerning the antibodies). After that, I shot for four months, which was the time for his next inoculation. In the end, I made it six months. I would have never made it that long if not for the help of Joe.

I give my man a lot of credit for rising above stereotypes and putting our child's best interest and our commitment to our decisions first. We both agreed we wanted to breastfeed him, so WE actually were usually a man can't say he helped breastfeed, but he did. All of our night feedings went with me pumping while he fed. While he was home with us in the beginning this was our normal routine; he did seventy-five percent of the actual feedings to alleviate some stress for me. After he went back to work, this changed and it was a lot harder to continue with a hungry or needy baby all day and to have to fit in pumps. However, that was mainly because the milk supply was so sensitive to supply and demand, if I was held up somewhere and did not express when needed, I lost milk. Then it was double sessions to make up the difference.

At the six-month mark an interesting thing happened: my pump broke. It was amazing it survived that long (some fifteen hundred pumps), (go electric, definitely worth the investment and cuts your pumping time down). Mind you I taped the thing back together, but took this as a clue to begin the weaning process. So just like weaning from the breast I took one pump out a day per week over the course of six weeks, so I was down to only three ounces a day when I finally hung up the pump. This helped with engorgement and Noah was able to ease into eating more and more formula. By the last week he was having one big (six ounce) bottle every morning and was hungry about an hour later, I knew then to wrap it up, he didn't need it anymore and has been very happy and thriving on formula and then solids. We started him on rice cereal around the same time-this way he wasn't losing anything, just changing.

For me this was the best thing I could do: feed my baby the way I wanted, (with some sacrifice on my part). Nevertheless, what is motherhood without sacrifice? I am not saying everyone should run out and do this, if not successful at breastfeeding, others may be able to try longer than I did and most people I know aren't as small as me either. If I were bigger or if he were smaller things may have been different also. Moreover, of course as I have learned, formula does not cause tail or horn growth. There is something to be said for taking control of your decisions and your life. I normally do not let things get in my way, sometimes I have to take a longer road, sometimes a bumpier one, but always the road I choose to walk.

Sometimes it is longer because I do not listen to myself. People always say hindsight is 20/20 and when I think back to the beginning of all this I remember how I knew something was wrong right from the start. And having been someone who has always "known things" I should have paid better attention to myself. I knew my parents were divorcing before they did, I have known a song is on the radio before I turn it on, when someone is about to call me or is calling me. Once I was lying on my bed and suddenly thought, I have to go into the living room fifteen seconds later I am standing out there asking myself why am I out here? And the overhead ceiling fan lamp suddenly crashed down on the bed I was laying on.

So when Noah was born, I knew something was wrong, or missing-an instinct that maybe he was overcooked or something. Over the next several years I found out I was right that there was something wrong, despite everyone telling me not to worry.

But as any mother will tell you, worrying is part of your job after all. Worry doesn't have to be an all-encompassing fear either, it doesn't have to invade your life, it doesn't even have to be something worth worrying about. So chances are, every mother has had thoughts and concerns regarding her children or her own abilities. I personally believe worry is normally unnecessary when it comes to something all-encompassing or running your life, or even if it occupies much of your thoughts. For if you worry about things that never happen, you just wasted all that time and energy on nothing. And if you worry about things that do happen, well you could have waited until it happened and up until then lived in blissful ignorance.

When Noah's first birthday approached but no first words I worried. But I was told, early walker late talker. When he was going on 2 and still only had maybe 10 words, I was told he's too busy to bother with talking,

"Oh he is a boy and boys don't always talk when they are supposed to". One of my well-meaning friends told me

My Grandmother said, "He sounds cute" to the way he made up his own language.

And of course my favorite that I heard from everyone and their mother, "early walker, late talker".

So his language is not really delayed because he's a boy and boys mature slower and of course the whole walking early thing. He did walk at nine months of age, crawling just frustrated him. This worried me too, but my dad told me I was the same way also never crawled, just stood up and walked one day. He also said I started talking at about seven months and hasn't shut up since. So why is it that I developed an extensive vocabulary by the time I was two, but Noah was not really talking and whatever he would say, he would never say again?

During one of Joe's company dinners a puzzle-pieced flag went up.

Joe and I have never been able to get out much; Noah was a surprise to a new romantic relationship (though we had been friends for six years prior) and as we all know after a baby, unless you have a nanny or very eager new grandparents living nearby, you are in baby jail that first year. Frankly, I was way too tired to care really, or complain about how seldom we got out. With the constant feeding schedule, and the fact he didn't sleep more than two-three hours in a row, going out was more of a chore.

But one night we had the company dinner for the holidays where the staff was taken out to a very nice steak house. So we got dressed up and headed over the bridge into Philadelphia to the Capital Grill Steak House, which is a huge place, very elegant without being too stuffy, simple designs with dark wood and light walls, and the wonderful smell of steak. Even during a brief period of my life where I went near vegan, I still loved that smell. We sat at linen clothed tables with proper table settings and ordered our food and chatted with each other. A lot of "Shop Talk", and people swapping kid stories. "So was Noah upset when you left?" Joe's boss's wife asked

"Not Noah, he doesn't have a serious interest in us or in any of his toys even. I guess you would say he is emotionally bankrupt." I replied

They found that amusing for some reason, but later on I thought about it. I didn't really think that was so funny- weren't babies supposed to be interested in their parents? Maybe he was, but I just couldn't tell.

Typical children look at their parents in wonder-they are expressive and so eager for you to teach them. But Autistic kids do not often look at us, let alone gaze into our eyes asking for the secrets of the universe, maybe because they already know it. it is still one of the biggest differences. I have often heard other parents exchange lists of what they find is the best part of being a parent. And at the top of the list is the social exchange between parent and child, the thirst for knowledge, the joy they feel knowing their child is looking to them to learn, and how they respond to what they are taught. This is usually followed by all of the fun activities they share and playing with their kids. Autism Spectrum Disorder or ASD kids lack this all completely or are very limited in it, which takes all of that wonder away and replaces it with much work with the hopes of an even higher reward that you are never certain will come.

The Best Laid Plans

Sometimes in life, you are given a crap hand, an unfair, unjust and undeserved situation or even an assault on your life. These are the things that happen, to which there was no way to change. You could not have chosen differently, for it was not something that was a bad choice.

In 2003 we purchased our home and had to sell Joe's previous home, one that we did share for the first 18 months of Noah's life. It was not an ideal place to raise a child, it was a one bedroom house that needed a lot of work, it was great for him, and he had a tenant upstairs. The house would have been too costly and then too big to convert. Noah's room was the front "sun porch". It had nine windows but was heated, in fact it had 3 cast iron radiators, but these are all things that don't scream "toddler's room". For all a mom can see is glass, and possible concussions.

The neighborhood was in a direct fly zone, which means the airplanes are beginning to land, so it sounds like they are possibly crashing on your house. If you are a light sleeper, I don't recommend this, it's not fun at 3 am. We also had raging alcoholics two doors down (who Joe happened to be related to), and who really liked our company unfortunately. Without the booze, they were fine people. After much consideration we had decided to sell.

It should have been simple, it was supposed to sell for about $108,000, after paying off the original mortgage and closing costs we were to walk away with just under $50,000.

But alas, just as this happened the law changed on underground storage tanks, the buyer could not get home owners insurance because of the tank during this transition.

The tank had to be tested to see if it could be abandoned, it did come out at low levels, but the state required that it be removed. The buyer was to put in a new heating system, so we weren't' worried about our tenant upstairs since it was spring. After all the results were done, and clean up began it turned out it was leaking for probably 10-15 years. This gave the buyer a legal out.

Later this summer the laws get settled, provisions and adjustments to insurances had to be in place by the state and we got a new realtor to find another buyer. This person was willing to pay more for the house, so it was going to work out even better. But alas, no. This deal fell through as well because of the clean-up costs.
Joe only owned this house for about 4 years at the time, but that didn't matter. It was our responsibility to clean it up. We could not qualify for any grants since it wasn't our primary residence anymore.

Eventually we do find a buyer, we pay the clean-up costs. Unfortunately at this point it took 2 years, so we were paying 2 mortgages, 2 sets of taxes and water bills, and since the house had an environmental problem, no tenants. As you can imagine, there would be debt.

I did what I could, and was able to pull in a few hundred a month, mostly to keep the credit cards paid, we used all our cash for the mortgages and taxes, water bills, utilities, and everything else went on credit cards. We had excellent credit at the time, so we had enormous limits. These were great in that they kept us from starving, we had gas in the car, diapers and necessities. We did not leave the house for one fun activity for 4 years.

We did not get any help. I tried, I went and applied for social services but we weren't poor enough by $200 a month, they did not count the other house. Too bad we could not have done the same. I had one friend give us a little bit of cash around the holidays one year, but otherwise no one gave us anything.

In the end it cost us well over $100,000.

I had a decent job before all this, so I had a lot of money saved, I worked too much to spend any of it. So I just saved. Since we had good credit at the time we qualified for a decent sized mortgage, but decided to play it conservatively and buy a smaller, starter home. One to live in for 5-7 years, we'd sell this house during that, refinance to a 20 year, it was a great plan. This was how everything began before we found out Noah had Autism. So needless to say, we were already a bag of stress and exhausted. We had no idea Noah was going to be disabled, need more space and how expensive that would all be. We had no idea this would affect our future so much, and to this day.

This is Jeopardy

"This is *Jeopardy*......and here's your host Alex Trebeck" Noah makes his declaration like he does most nights Jeopardy is on, hands a-flapping like a very excited little bird.

"Noah, do you like *Jeopardy*?" I ask him while he is staring at the TV.

No response

"Noah, Noah do you like *Jeopardy*?" I ask again in case he didn't hear me, though most people can, I am not known to be soft-spoken.

Again no response, I repeat again and he makes some noises and then says

"This is *Jeopardy*"

So naturally, I figure maybe if this is *Jeopardy* I should be giving him the answer so then he can give me the question.

"Noah's favorite TV show."

"What is *Jeopardy.*"

Well that is close. No wonder he likes this show so much, it gives you all the answers.

It is sometime in October or November of 2005; Noah is three and still not really talking. He is not making any sentences nothing more than "milk", "juice", or "TV". Everyone I talk to, including his doctor, still thinks that this is perfectly ok. I admit even though I have been feeling that something was just off for a long time, I shrugged off some of my own doubts to being a first time mom. But now more time has passed and even more things seem off.

When Noah was three he had been to all of the normal well baby visits and I still received the same excuses as to why he seemed delayed. I was more demanding because now there is still a list of other problems I have noticed. Things I probably didn't complain about because I am normally very patient and tolerant.

One of the main things I noticed was he would leave the room when I tried to play with him. I would follow him to the other room, and then he would eventually leave that one, never wanting to play with any of his toys or games with me. Even older than three, he behaved this way.

I first thought this was my fault, maybe I don't know how to play with him, completely forgetting I have been around kids most of my life, I was heavily involved in theater, and, oh yeah and I used to be a clown. But somehow, I the entertainer am to blame for not being able to entertain MY OWN child.

I did eventually realize it wasn't me. Then there were the other oddities; he never pointed at anything, never brought a toy to me to look at or share attention. Never looked for a hug or gave any affection, hardly made eye contact, didn't want to be held, hated loud noises, and fluorescent lighting. He would have long frustrating tantrums about what seemed to be nothing, things you couldn't understand, such as cutting up a hotdog as opposed to keeping it whole, or drawing the wrong thing.

And when he was very frustrated he would bang his head on the floor. I would share my concerns with the doctors, our parents, and other parents, even people at the grocery store. People would either find it amusing and cute, or say there is nothing wrong with him. So really what they were saying was, Noah was just holding back, and all the odd behaviors were just bad parenting? But what about the constant lining up of objects, cars, crayons, Tupperware, pieces of toys? Surely this isn't normal and can't be attributed to bad parenting?

Still, despite the fact I am a first time mom, I still added the fact he couldn't talk or communicate well to a list of peculiarities that was growing.

This night, of watching Jeopardy and Lingo (also a favorite) caused Noah's emotions to run the spectrum from being very joyful of his programs to being so frustrated he was banging his head on the floor. Noah is sitting on the wood floor of our living room enthralled in TV one minute, and then suddenly making some yelling and grunting sounds the next.

"Whoa buddy, what's wrong?" I asked him, even though I knew he wouldn't answer.

Suddenly he took his head and started to bang it right on the floor. I immediately put my hand in between his head and the hard wooden floor.

"What was that all about?" Joe asked a little freaked out, while Noah was still screaming and crying and not wanting me to touch him in any way.

"I don't know, maybe we should give him a bath and see if he calms down" I said, remembering the lavender baby bath that we have been using to help him settle.

Noah couldn't ask or say what was bothering him, it stressed him out to the point that he wants to bang his head in. Surely we all know things that make us feel like that; generally we don't do it, but we can talk about it. But here is this child that cannot express what he is feeling with his own words, more and more often he spoke in this bizarre dialect cut from movies, video games, and TV shows. And now he could recite the beginning of Jeopardy verbatim. This is why we started to call him Rain man and that rather Un-PC joke, was a catalyst, a little voice that asked the question and then also answered it.

Very soon after this I scheduled a "well baby visit". The original three-year-old visit in May or June, Noah was sick so it wasn't exactly a "well baby" visit and his normal doctor did not see him. So no matter what concerns I had then, they were only pacified by the fact he had an illness, so that must have explained his behavior at the time of the visit, at least to the doctor. So in the fall of 2005, when we back for the real well baby visit. The doctor did respond differently to my concerns, scribbling off some names of specialists in the system and said something about a spectrum disorder. She never used the word Autism, so for all I knew a spectrum disorder had something to do with hallucinating colors. I spent any free time I had which was next to none calling all of the places she referred, all of whom had long waiting lists for almost two years.

Thankfully I found a hospital about an hour and half from here that was willing to see us in three weeks. Noah is now three and a half years old or forty-two months, time is ticking on like a noisy clock in my ears. What a waste of precious time that could have been better spent. He could have been on the right path much sooner if anyone took my concerns more seriously

December 2005 Off to Diagnosis Land

"I'll stand up next to a mountain and chop it down with the edge of my hand... maybe I will pick up the pieces and make an island."
~Jimi Hendrix

I have never been a fan of the New Jersey turnpike, despite the fact it is a central freeway that can lead you to almost any destination in NJ or to NY. It's heavily traveled, full of tractor-trailers, and by sheer probability some of the worst drivers all in one big hurry. Which is funny because there are no lights, so even if you obey the speed limit, you can get anywhere you need way faster than driving any of the other numerous roads to your destination. But for New Jersians it's just not fast enough.

We pile in the car on a December morning in 2005 on our way to Children's Specialized Services Hospital to see one Doctor Harris. I know that at the end of this road is not just a building with doctors, but also an answer.

Finally someone can tell us, (hopefully tell us) what is going on with Noah. What is a spectrum disorder?
But most importantly we will have the information we need to start to make things better.
Noah is not a huge fan of long car rides, so now neither am I. I used to like the long ride, even though the turnpike has claimed the lives of many including a best friend of my own. Noah is making noises to himself and kicking my seat the whole way.

After being on the road for about two hours we pull into this modern looking building and find our way to the receptionist desk. The waiting area is full of sensory styled toys, the usual magazines and other waiting patients. For the first time in my life, I finally made the connection as to why we are called patients, it's because you really need a lot of patience to sit there as long as they make you wait. And little did I know, we would be waiting here two to three times longer than your typical doctor waiting period.

Noah is restless from the long journey, wandering about and touching things, anything he can touch. He has a fondness for light switches and begins to go turn them on and off. The people here are used to it I guess, because they are not fazed at all.
"Noah, come over here, we don't have to wait too much longer."

He still appears deaf, but with some guidance he gravitates over to some of the sensory tables on the walls. There is another little boy in the room now, about the same size as Noah. He is also grumbling to himself, not looking at anyone and touching things. For whatever reason, Noah and this child decided to pal around the room together. Not really talking to each other, but still in each other's company. Reminded me of that saying birds of a feather, and they did not need words. Touch spin, touch spin was the main thing they are doing.

After an hour he had enough. "Go Now!!" he said. Hey at least he said something, and it was two words.

Screaming and crying follows as the nurse comes out with some bubbles to lead Noah down the enchanted path to diagnosis land. He is interested in the bubbles and following but still crying the whole way. At this point I am kind of ticked off myself, not only had we endured the long stress radiating drive, but the last hour of constant following and correcting, ending with a tantrum just not that fun.

They weigh Noah and all the other usual things and send us to the next room where we wait some more for the doctor. At first Noah looked around the room and was interested in the little black covers for the Otoscope used for examining ears. After not being satisfied with one he is upset again and wanting to leave, turning off the

lights. He climbs into a cabinet under a sink and is happy with hiding out in there.
The door opens again and in walks our doctor.
"Hello, I am Doctor Harris, sorry we had to have you wait so long, but we need to see how long it takes him to recover from being upset"

I figure this is test number one and we introduce ourselves.

"So what brought you here?' She asks us after the typical medical information exchange.

"Besides the car? "I joked (ah how I love my obvious humor). "I guess that's a loaded question, Noah's pediatrician gave us a referral for something called a spectrum disorder, but didn't explain what that was."

"Can you describe what you're seeing?"

"Well, he doesn't say much, I counted once, and I think he has maybe twenty to forty words. He repeats things he hears from *Jeopardy* or *Peter Pan*, he also repeats back the last word or two you say. He doesn't like to play with us, though he has been friendly when we take him for walks in his stroller, smiling at people. He hit most of his milestones but never crawled. He did have virtually no words and just babbled when he was twelve months old, but most things he said he never said again. He doesn't play with his toys, he just takes them apart and plays with the pieces or lines them up in rows, sometimes he varies it and makes designs. I have been completely unable to potty train him at all, he has seemed unready. None of the signs have been there. But the worst part is he gets extremely agitated over things you can't identify and sometimes he bangs his head on the floor or on us."

"What kind of activities does he like to do besides taking things apart?"

"Well he likes to rip up paper, or spin himself. He spins himself a lot; he also literally bounces off the walls and furniture. He also likes to watch TV, and he usually does all those things while he is watching TV."

Dr. Harris spent over an hour talking with us; she let Noah play in the cabinet with her flashlight. Then it was his turn to be examined.

"Noah, how old are you?" Dr. Harris asked.

"You," Noah answered.
He was mostly interested in the doctor's tools, the light sockets, and all those things that are part of a doctor's office. The doctor was unable to get him structured enough to implement all of the cognitive testing; she was able to accomplish some of it. He held a pencil with a palmer grasp, (which means, holding it in a fist) could not copy any item, and only lightly scribbled. His Language skills on the CLAMS test (Clinical Linguistic and Auditory Milestone Scales) was that of a twenty-two month level (Noah was forty-two months at the time)

The diagnostic labels and criteria for autism and the spectrum it encompasses have changed a lot over the past fifty years. Right now the most widely accepted diagnostic tool used in the US is in the American Psychiatric Association Diagnostic and Statistical Manual for Mental Disorders, Fourth Edition, commonly referred to as DSM-IV-TR CRITERIA. It is a list of twelve yes or no questions divided into three categories. To receive a diagnosis of Pervasive Developmental Disorder or PDD, there would have to be at least six out of the twelve criteria answered positively, and at least two of those have to fall in the social category. The other two categories are communication and play skills.

Noah's results were positive for ten out of twelve of the questions. Three were in the social category, all four of the communication category and three out of four of the play category. He was able to demonstrate he knew his colors and could identify some body parts. But mostly, Noah pretty much just went from item to item, really fascinated with all of the wall sockets.

"He jargons a lot, do you find he is self- talking or talking to imaginary friends often?' asked Dr. Harris

I told her yes, and wondered how she knew that, I didn't know any of his "self-talking" was a symptom.

"How is he with auditory stimuli, regular sounds" she asked as she was going down a checklist

"Oh, he hates loud talking, the vacuum cleaner, the blender, fire trucks. He usually covers his ears and leaves the room"

"I want you to go to your school's child study team and have them do full evaluations of these areas. Language communication disorder; disordered social interaction, narrow interests, with significant interest in dark places, lights and mechanical things; significant sensory issues with loud sounds, lights and possible oral motor texture intolerance. They are required by law to provide services for Noah. "

"All of these symptoms fall into what is known as PDD or Pervasive Developmental Disorder."

She didn't say the word Autism at this point, however all of the pamphlets, literature and hotline numbers she gave me did. I have never been a fan of math, but I have always been able to put two and two together. Despite her having spared us the "word", after all of the study team evaluations were complete; the label Noah was assigned was Autistic. It wasn't until later when I was looking into these things did I understand why she didn't say the word Autism. Apparently there has been a great many of parents that are very uncomfortable with the word; it gives them a feeling of hopelessness and lack of control. So much so they refer to it as the A word. I

would never refer to it as the A word, I already have a word that is being taken up by that title.
I understand we live in a world where we must label everything, and it doesn't matter to me what you call it. At least I had a word to use on Internet searches; Noah was still Noah, now at least I know there is a reason for him being such an unpleasant child. Now his behavior is a symptom, it's the autism I can be mad at; it's the Autism that is the devil, not him.

"So what can we do?" I asked after trying to digest a lot of the information.

"Every child is different-most parents will try different therapies and see which ones work the best. Your starting place should be with your school district. They are required by law to give a free and appropriate education to all children, and when your child is of preschool age, they must do evaluations if you request them. This will determine that he needs special services. Do this right away. They have to schedule an Individual Educational Plan or IEP meeting and begin evaluations with in ninety days. I want you to come back here in three months to see what you were able to find out."

We finished out meeting with our new best friend Dr.Harris, it was an engaging experience, and she spent nearly two hours with us that first day. We all hugged and headed out the door into another room where she gave us all the pamphlets. Noah was mesmerized by the machine in there that is kind of like a medical craftmatic bed, for examinations. I have seen these numerous times in doctors' offices and never realized they did anything, somehow Noah knew and immediately pressed the button to turn it on.

"Well its official, he has now passed the PDD test." Dr. Harris stated with some humor in her voice "Every one of our kids turns that on at some point here."

I liked how she referred to him and all the other PDD-kids as their kids. And then I thought, gee such a simple test, which would've taken five minutes. Not the hours that went to getting here, being here. The schools should invest in this machine; it would save a ridiculous amount of money on evaluations.

Finally we had a diagnosis and began the long process of going through your child study team to get services. At this point I felt such relief to finally know what it was and now I can begin to fix it. People will tell you that once you get the diagnosis the world will suddenly stop and you're going to grieve. But for me, it was a relief! I finally had proof all the problems I was having with him had a reason, which now means there is a solution. I felt empowered to be able to help. My grief is reserved for the long months of winter.

There is anything wrong with feeling sad your child is ill. My husband was pretty depressed and angry, but wouldn't admit or talk about it much, so it just came out in inappropriate ways. Which is funny because that is the same for these kids.

But it's not necessary to feel destroyed or let down because of it. It's a challenge, and whether or not you're religious, it's nice to think we are only given what we can handle, whether we know it or not. I know other people who, if they had a child like Noah, I am not sure how they would handle it, or how the child would handle these parents handling them.

Of course, this was how I felt. Joe on the other hand was silent the car ride home. I think his journey that began in this moment was more typical to a lot of parents. Things they envisioned for their child and themselves are slipping away, I tried to remind him that whatever parents envision, it is never fair to any kid, let alone one that has a medical problem. Really nothing was different; we just had a name to call all of these attributes that are Noah. But things were better, because at least we now can find a road map to navigate these problems. Otherwise there would be no improvements, things would just continue to be frustrating and suck.

I spent some time on the Internet later looking up PDD, and "spectrum disorder," both referred to Autism, which is stated as a complex neurological disorder effecting communication, language and social skills- pretty much everything she wrote up on her script for us to give to the child study team. Basically, Autism presents with repetitious or odd behaviors. Due to an imbalance in the brain with impairment largely on the right side, some children have overactive left-brains; others may have a combination of specific areas of deficits alongside areas of high functioning.

In Noah's case without using all the scientific terminology, it is the areas of the brain that cover decision making, socialization, anxiety, alertness, and mostly the ability to differentiate among conflicting thoughts. With this being impaired, learning things such as language becomes a daunting task. And good and bad behavior takes on different meaning.

Nearly all autistic children have sensory integration processing disorders, meaning where one or multiple senses are over sensitive, other parts of the nervous system are under stimulated, causing the child to be restless or hyper because they can't feel parts of their body, also sometimes causing them to scream or be fearful to bright lights or loud noises, because those lights and noises are a different form of pain. It is not a physical pain like an upset stomach or a headache, though both of these can happen as the day wears on. It is your brain telling you you're in pain, and since there is not physical pain, there is nothing you can do to tell your brain otherwise. I have experienced this myself. From all of the stress of this situation over the years, and other stresses my own problems processing certain sounds and sensitivity to light occur when my system is over-burdened. I still don't know exactly what it is like to be a child with a spectrum disorder, but now I have an idea of part of it, and just knowing that part is enough to get my sympathies.

During this, Noah was set up to get some labs done and I wrote my letter to the school to request the four different evaluations Dr. Harris recommended, while continuing my research on various therapies I could try at home. Upon getting the labs back and seeing where enzymes were off and too high, I most seriously considered taking dairy out of his diet. I had read about a gluten-free, Casein-free diet. And since some of his enzymes on his labs were way off, I thought it was worth a try.

I learned the main point of the diet is for people who cannot fully digest dairy products and wheat products. The peptides do not break down in these kids and they float around in their system causing digestive problems and this interferes with learning. Dairy acts like an opiate, like heroin, where the child cannot learn and is more hyper and out of sorts with themselves. It blocks pain messages, creates confusion, and reduces the desire for social interaction. All of these things are part of

Noah, including a reduced appetite, bowel problems, eczema and constant redness in his cheeks and ears. We eliminated dairy for three days and it would be difficult to say whether or not his behavior was truly different because you know you're doing something that you are hoping is going to work. What made the most sense was to give him some ice cream a few days later and then see if there was anything worth noting. After eating the ice cream he was extra stimmy and later was incredibly irritable for a couple of days. It was similar to watching someone detoxify off of drugs or alcohol. We repeated this exercise a few times to be certain. Over the next month we stuck to the dairy free diet and watched his belly stop protruding, and the inflammation in his face disappear. He stimmed less also, and was more even, it wasn't like a miracle cure, but there was a definite physical and emotional difference. One that was quantifiable with data, one that I could see.

By February he had been off the white stuff and we began the elimination of gluten. From everything I read it seemed gluten would take anywhere from six to eight months to fully leave his system, so it would be difficult to gage how effective it was or necessary. And, unfortunately, it is not the same as dairy if there is an infraction or even to intentionally give him something and see if there was a difference, since it could lay in his system for another month.

On our return visit to doctor Harris we talked about his diet.

"I have read about it and some of my patient's parents are attempting this diet, but right now there are no conclusive studies completed. So I can't tell you if it will work or not." Dr. Harris said

"I know it's anecdotal, but all things start somewhere, so I figure it's worth a try." I replied

"Well the truth is we would all be healthier eating this way, so it wouldn't hurt to do it, if you are willing to make the necessary sacrifices."

Two years later, Dr. Harris said to me she can't dispute the results of this diet for those that need it, and has seen the benefits that have resulted from it in her other patients.

We told her we started the process with the school, and the evaluations were to begin in March. We were reading on a therapy called Floor time and started learning about how to provide it ourselves.

I personal feel that Autism is not as complicated as it seems-it really can be summed up as an imbalance in the brain and nervous system. And balance is something I believe in and have had, thinking of it in these simple terms I also find it not so overwhelming. Of course many people will tell you there is no cure and all you have is hope, and maybe some slight improvements. Noah will always be odd, likely need medication will probably never speak, will be withdrawn into himself more and more.

Not that I believe all of that. I do fully believe he can "recover" because autism is just a neurological disorder mostly on one side of the brain. And the brain is an amazing organ with much placity, Neurons fire where they have fired before, and the brain will allow parts to die off that aren't used.

So the challenge is getting those neurons to fire as often as possible so they will start doing so on their own. Autism is truly a battle against time, something I am quite comfortable with. Since I have previously worked in the Transportation industry, which is completely about time and what a limited resource it is, it is one of the few things a person cannot buy no matter how wealthy they are.

Change is Going to Come

Dr. Harris was very clear about calling the school right away and writing a formal letter requesting the evaluations she had written on a script. They included an evaluation for Sensory integration dysfunction, Speech and communication disorder, fine motor and motor planning, and behavioral and social problems. We had seen her on December 9th so I called the school the next business day.

I hadn't read the horror stories about school districts and IEP's at this point. And there are absolutely more horror stories than positive ones, which usually require the parents getting lawyers and having to sue the district for them to just do what is right. But since Noah would be going into the same school district I went through my whole life, I wasn't concerned. I enjoyed my time in school in Maple Shade, was heavily involved but didn't have any issues that required extra services. My sister did, and when I remembered that put me more on my guard, but didn't know any better at the time.

I called the main line for the school district and found the extension for the child study team; there I was transferred to someone who was the main caseworker.

"Hi, I have a script from my son's Neurodevelopmental Pediatrician requesting some evaluations to be done?"

" Well the first thing you have to do is send in a short letter listing the evaluations you want done and then mail it to our office here in Maple Shade. We are about to go on the Christmas holiday so can you mail it after the New Year?"

I agreed to do so; not thinking it was that big of a deal, until later when I realized they have a time window to respond and set up the evaluations, as well as a 90 day window to begin services. If I had mailed it right away, as Dr. Harris had nearly demanded, that meant they would have had to begin services in mid-March, holiday or no holiday. But since I did as they asked, that gave them almost another month.

Evaluations began with a parade of professionals, a psychologist, a learning consultant, a behavior therapist, a speech consultant, an occupational therapist, and the social worker that took the original call. Most of these were held in our home, and we took Noah to the school for the speech and occupational therapy or OT evaluation.

Little Squares with Colors

Evaluations are a tricky thing-you always want your child to do well, but in this case you don't want them to have a great day and do too well, for fear of not getting the therapy you need for them. One of the interesting aspects of Autism spectrum disorders or ASD's is how a child can come in and out of it; sometimes they blend in like any other preschooler. All preschoolers are weird in their own way, when else in life can you go around saying inappropriate things, lifting up your clothing in public, or having a tantrum without being sent to the place with the padded walls? The difference between the "typicals" and the ASD kids is a fine line, because all kids are capable of going into their own worlds but ASD kids do it more often and stay there longer. Typical kids get distracted, they don't always listen when they're being talked to, and they drive their parents crazy in their own ways.

There is also a difference between a tantrum and a meltdown; all kids have tantrums- over-the-top behavior for means of manipulation. Sometimes they are just angry. And though all kids can have meltdowns; a meltdown is different. It appears as crying, screaming or "bad behavior", but it is a result of sensory overload. There is no actually desired result, these kids don't' want anything except to feel better. Typical kids also want to play with their parents and other kids, they show affection, they may like to spin themselves or jump around, but they don't primarily do that.

Little Squares with Colors

Since we were not willing to wait on the school, we had begun our own therapy, prior to these evaluations so Noah was already making progress before any of the official people saw him.

The first evaluation was the Occupational therapist at the school since she had a lot of equipment to work with there, plus it would be a good measure of his ability to regulate in a different setting. We came into the room, which is in the school he would possibly be attending at some unknown future date. Noah immediately went in explorer mode while I did the introductions since stuff is more interesting than people.

The therapist was young and warm. I liked her right away.

"Hi my name is Sydney, " she said as we shook hands.

"Hi, I am Christine and that is Noah, pillaging"

She was able to get some eye contact from him here and there; I am starting to wonder if Noah is more like Sami our cat maybe the more eye contact the better the person?

Sydney had a bunch of tasks for him to perform. Hop on one foot, balance on one foot, jump up and down, string beads on a pipe cleaner, push the green button, and put the paper in the blue box. He did everything that was asked of him, but maybe not as well as he was "supposed to" As usual he was highly distracted jumping from one activity to another every few minutes. "Is this about the same as his attention span at home?" she asked

"For the most part when he is playing on his own, if you can call it that. When we have table time, he can sit for five to ten minutes. But I have the TV on also. Table time is just him and me with some activity books working on bigger and smaller, his shapes and colors. He mostly likes it."

Noah has now seen the globe of the Earth in the room and has the look of captivation and capture in his eyes. He was not okay with not touching it.

We talked for a while about Noah's habits, the sounds he didn't like, the ones he seemed to make and seek out. How he throws his body around and falls out of chairs, how he bumps into things and doesn't notice, and his eating habits.

She used a test called the Peabody for Developmental Motor scales, a standardized test used to asses motor skills in a typically developing 0-72 month population. Noah was 46 months at the time of testing and scored in the 1%. His visual motor integration was higher in the 25% category but when combined it was still the 1%. There were more areas she studied and I actually did not realize how many areas of sensory integration exist. The thought alone made me overwhelmed; suddenly Noah's need for dark places seemed more like brilliance than a disability.

Overall, he was in a definite difference in 13 of the 23 categories, followed by 6 in probably difference and scored typically in 4 of the 23 categories. This is not good, but did require help, and that's all that matters at this point.

In May of 2006 Noah had his Speech and Language evaluation, which was done in the school conference room. Noah was highly energetic when he entered the very bland room. As usual he did not greet the person already in the room or made any eye contact with them. He began wandering about and explored the room, but was most interested in the light switches and outlets.

He did not speak about spontaneously, nor did he respond naturally. He spoke his normal parrot speak of repeating thing he has heard on TV, which I learned is called Echolia (which is not a digestive disorder, that's E.coli.) She watched him line up the toys that were there in an organized fashion, and when she would have to ask him any questions he would get very irritated that she disrupted his little world.

"His expressive language would be that of a 2 year old, but his receptive actually is more of a 1 year old," The therapist stated.

"Well that explains a lot," I mused but I only found this amusing.

"Some of his skills are near a three year old level. He is about to be four though correct? I would recommend he is seen at least three times a week for 20-minute sessions, mostly individual with one to two being group sessions of no more than five children."

We said our goodbyes and were about to leave but Noah was not willing to give up one of the toys that had piqued his interest. He had no goodbyes for the therapist as he did not understand why he wasn't taking the toy he was playing with. He was playing with it after all; that in his mind would make the toy his, since he liked it.

The parade of therapists continued, they all said similar things. How cute he is, how bright, what a joy to work with and a pleasure. How energetic, they also said other things I didn't understand like "Palmer grasp", "hyperlexic," "manding" and "self-stimulatory behaviors". I of course looked all of these up and have a fine understanding of them now, they are in order: Autism to English - Holds pencil or crayon in fist, can sight read at an earlier age than normal, asking for items, and all the spinning, hand flapping and banging his body around - also known as a "stim" for short for self-stimulatory behaviors (which honestly, just sounds dirty).

Little Squares with Colors

As of June 2006 we were still waiting on the behavior therapist to complete all of the evaluations; once we had hers done we could sit down for the IEP meeting. It has been over six months at this point, twice the legal limit.

Finally the day came for the last of evaluations and we had Noah all primed and ready, plus we had been working with him for six months, and he had been on the diet for about four months now. Already he has improved, so this evaluation was a bit more nerve-wracking.

"Hello Noah," she said very brightly (and he actually gave her a hug). " My name is Becky, I want to play with you for a little while."

He looked over whatever stuff she had, but decided he liked her electronic toys best. He was most interested in her Palm Pilot, cell phone camera and I Pod. Typical modern technology and to this day we have yet to purchase any of it due to the high cost of Noah's therapies.

"iPod," Noah said when looking that gadget over.

"When did he start to read?" Becky asked.

"Probably a year ago, I noticed he could read one day when I had some *Wawa* sugar packets in the trash can and he said the word *Wawa*. So then I made a list of other words he may know and had him read them to me.

So he could read most colors, the word *Pooh*, the word *play* and about twenty more."

"That is what we call Hyperlexic, since he can read them phonetically by sounding them out. This is a processing strength but also a weakness since he may not comprehend all that he reads." Becky then picks him up and holds him in the air over her head, which at first he loves. But then he wants down.

"Tell me you want down" she says to Noah.

He starts to get upset and whiney and blurting out " DOWN! DOWN!"

"No, say I want down." She reminds him. I am also familiar with this game, and I hope she is prepared for the after show.

A few minutes later he strings together all three words, and she puts him down. "Good job Noah, "she says

He then picks up the closest item - a Winnie the Pooh puzzle and wails it near her head.

"Noah, we don't throw, say you're sorry." I firmly remind him.

He is all red in the face and just manages to grunt at me.

"Okay, then it's time out in your room for four minutes" I say. He suddenly regains his ability of speech by protesting NO the whole way down the hallway to his room. I come back and apologize on his behalf.

"No, it's okay, that's actually good to see how he calms down." She says. Again with the calming down tests, these tests would be better if they came with a free massage for the parents afterward. Unfortunately we would have to move to the United Kingdom to receive them.

"We normally put him in Time Out in his room, since it's dark in there. That seems to work best. When we did it in the hallway or made him stand in the corner he would just get more worked up and wind up banging his head on the wall." I tell her. He does calm down and eventually rejoins us where he cleans up his mess.

When it's over and we look over all of their reports. They all agree Noah would benefit from a home-program for the summer and fall, eventually transitioning him into the disabled preschool in the spring. He will receive Applied Behavior Analysis, Speech and Occupational Therapy in the home.

Our school district does not make up a horror story compared to some thing's I have read that occurs in cold, unfeeling rooms with not fully present parties. There were mistakes, disappointments and stress that will come up later. I can say that the people we have worked with here have their hearts in the right places. They genuinely want to help kids, but it's not all up to them. Unfortunately when you live in a state that has multiple districts and multiple counties, there are multiple people in charge of running them. And it is those powers that decide how much funding a school gets and give the final okay when trying a new therapy or when you need to think outside the box. They are the ones that decide if a school can have an Autism class or not, and decide how many kids can be capped in a classroom.

There has been much improvement regarding Special Needs education, however there is still more advancement needed. Because of the very nature of our life with Noah, and the lack of assistance we do get, there is no time left at this point for us to get out there and change anything with the state or community. If we had more help we would be able to do this, but if we had more help, than they would be doing their jobs and that would mean there wouldn't be a need. I don't find empty complaining very rewarding in the long run, though venting is necessary. I do the best I can to be pro-active with our school district and getting them to think outside the box. It is good for Noah that I am like this; otherwise I suppose I wouldn't be very involved with helping him.

Out in the Dark is a Beckoning Candle.

Autism affects nearly every area of Noah and our family's daily life. Keeping it very interesting, never knowing what to expect. One minute you're watching a movie and the next you're cleaning up applesauce he suddenly threw on the floor, which in the end just gives you clean floors, since you have to mop them up for something or other every day.

One fun time when he is four going on five his diaper goes missing, when I ask him about it he says, "I took it off, I clean it up". I find out he put it in his ball pit, and there it was. I am super excited because a year ago he would have never been able to answer those questions. So Autism ultimately makes you grateful for the everyday, the little triumphs, and those moments when you have practiced something a hundred times and he finally gets it.

Little Squares with Colors

In the early spring of 2006 while waiting for the evaluations to finish and the services to start we begin Floor Time, which is also known as the DIR model by Dr. Stanley Greenspan. The DIR stands for Developmental Individual difference Relationship based model and is used in conjunction with other therapies of kids with ASD's.

It is an important foundation to build on because it involves the relationship between the child and people. Most of these kids are not as interested in people as they are things. For Noah it was this case, he could spend most of his time by himself lining up toys, pulling tires off of cars, shredding paper. He was most at peace by himself and could spend the whole day that way if I let him, I know he prefers it, but instinctively I am always talking to him. Probably annoying him, but it is for his own good.

I had read several books on Greenspan's work, and took a workshop as well. But since we were not financially blessed we never were able to meet with Mr. Greenspan himself, so conducting our own research and learning it ourselves was the next best thing. The main point of DIR is to follow your child's natural interests building circles of communication one at a time. You hiding a toy, child finding the toy is one circle, hiding your face and uncovering it is another circle. Moving on down the road and including basic communication such as you smile they smile, is one of the harder ones to make happen.

Frankly, it is a lot of the same games and activities parents and caregivers always do with their children. The same activities that Noah never would engage in, so there is a twist of course into how to get him engaged and more importantly, keep him there.

It was named Floor Time, because it largely takes place on the floor. After a child has developed more language this is transitioned to verbal work where you are having circles of communication. In the beginning it is a lot of crawling around with the child, hiding toys and finding them together, basically a very fast paced method of normal play. Hide and Seek on speed! Everything is more exaggerated than normal, making it more tiring, and this method requires doing multiple short sessions throughout the day, every day. So in our case it was about eight 20-30 minute sessions a day. This is still less than the previous breastfeeding challenge.

And for women out there who want to beat themselves up for not losing weight, regardless of not having time to eat and sweating on the floor for four hours every day for four months, I still did not lose a single pound. Stress is a bitch to hormones.

A typical session involves Noah in his playroom; taking one of his plush toys and hiding it.

"Where's the dog Noah?" I ask in this extremely high pitched cartoon voice

Noah turns from the shelves of books and looks at me, I then show him the dog and immediately hide it behind my back.

"Where did the dog go?" I say in same cartoon voice

Noah comes over and starts to look around my back.

"You found it," I say shaking it at him. Next I take the dog and hide it under a pillow on the couch. "Find the dog, find the dog." I chant like a hyper Mickey Mouse. Noah runs around looking for the dog and once he finds it I hide it again, this goes on for several sweaty minutes.

We make everything into a game, anything he does is a game, but it works because suddenly he is laughing and looking at us. Not just through us as he so often does, but right at us. Giggling and running around playing with us, which before he never wanted or maybe never was able to do.

We use other types of toys also, cars, PVC figures, anything he seems to be interested in and hide them so he can find them. We also use a lot of bubbles, and to this day I have a bottle of bubbles in every room. I purchase as many toys as we can afford, and later on when the behavior therapists start coming over they would bring more. The playroom was full with bins featuring a cornucopia of various sensory toys, and games. Even though it is neat, whenever my Grandmother visits she greets us with "look at all the toys" saying it in a disapproving way, she doesn't get it.

We somehow keep up this grueling schedule for four or five months until the official real therapists come in. At this point I feel he has a good foundation to build on and I want to move to the next step of having him respond verbally with imaginative play.

I spend about a month trying to teach him how to play with his stuffed toys. These are safe; they are the great building blocks for pretend play. They are soft, so if he gets frustrated and throws them at me or hits me with them, it's a lot more pleasant then when you are working with blocks or LEGO's. No weirdly shaped bruises with circle patterns.

Winnie the Pooh and all his "friends" are still to this day big friends of Noah's. I start off with just making Piglet talk to Roo. I figure we will just work on how you say Hi to someone. This is an important skill, he never really says hello to anyone when they come in or when we go anywhere. Often he runs and hides. So I begin with Roo asking, "How are you Piglet?" And then I would make Piglet answer, "I am okay". After modeling it for a while I wait to see if he will make Piglet answer, for a long time it is just a one-way conversation with Piglet and Roo sharing the same squeaky voice. But then after about a month, one fateful day Roo asks Piglet how he was.

This time Piglet finally answers in his own voice: "I'm Okay".

I feel like Rocky Balboa.

Voice in high-pitched Roo-like squeakiness " Great job Noah! You did it!"

"I'm Okay" Noah repeats again, eyes shining

This was a break through and a beginning of the use of imaginative play, as far as typical standards are concerned. Because it is not as if Autistic kids do not use their imagination when they play, we just don't know they are because of the language barrier.

Flash forward a year after this Noah is playing with some blocks, lining them up making them talk to each other, when I realize this is one of those things he always did but instead of words it is grunts and beeps.

"What are you doing Noah?" I asked him while he was in the middle of it." What are you playing?"

"These are robots. "he says proudly. Then the light goes on in my own mind

Now that Noah has more words I know that all the playing with parts was still representative of something and not just random like it appeared. Of course, robots! Oh they're dogs! Okay, all this time they were things, nobody asked, and he couldn't answer before.

Mona Lisa's and Mad Hatters
"I thank the lord for the people I have found"

After a long dramatic wait, in July of 2006 the official therapy finally begins. It only took seven months from the time I requested it for this to happen. It took the school six of these months to get all of the evaluations done, and sit down to have the first IEP meeting. The first meeting of many more to come from now until Noah is no longer in school or needs special services. From this point to the end of the school year of 2009, we had almost ten IEP meetings.

We had of course been implementing our own forms of therapy, but the professional Therapy began a few weeks after this meeting on July 5th. It was needed not only because they have more resources and knowledge than us, but also it is a break from giving constant therapy. My main belief all this time was to take every moment as a teaching moment, and when you live like that, you are always on, and there is no break except when you're sleeping.

Little Squares with Colors

The IEP is set to give Noah two hours of Occupational therapy, and one hour of Speech. The IEP also gives him a minimum of twenty-five hours of in home therapy with Behavior specialists from *Minding Manners*. The sessions are to be set up as two hour shifts twice a day, five days a week. Which we do for some time but this doesn't work well, since it takes too much time for the therapist to set up, clean up and get Noah engaged. So I arrange them to have three hour shifts all five days, and the remaining hours were ok to be two hour shifts. In the beginning the Behavioral specialists sent three different therapists throughout the week, and one consultant. This gives us six new faces to learn, six new personalities to adapt to. In the end Noah had worked with over thirteen different therapists during the two years we used them.

Minding Manners' job is to teach Noah more language and a lot of the basic information he should know at his age. He was four when this begins. They bring in laminated cards, lots of them. They have pictures of animals, emotions, objects, actions, colors, shapes, and sequencing. They bring a lot of games and toys, accompanied with great fun attitudes. Some of them were naturals and Noah just clicked with them. Their job is to teach, keep him engaged, teach him to sit and help keep his brain stimulated. Basically to expand and build upon the foundation we had laid. The results were amazing. Noah goes from about 50 words the equivalent of a two year old; when they begin and by the time he is six he went to having a vocabulary of a five year old and all of the basic knowledge of one.

Most of them are successful at keeping him engaged, but not all. That is one thing you will learn as you go through this, we were extremely blessed that the first group was a near perfect mix of personalities and styles. Kristen was a young college student about to graduate. Noah probably saw her like a big sister who was very fun, full of energy and was non-reactive when Noah would get into a mood and just wail on her.

"You do understand he beats on you because he likes you the most." I told her hoping she was not upset about Noah's latest attack.

She laughed and said she was used to it, Noah was a walk in the park compared to the 13-year-old girl she works with that was probably 150 pounds and was entering puberty.

Paige, was the same age as me, and most similar in style as my own. She was naturally bubbly and animated. Everything she said to Noah clicked with him, because she was always on, despite the obvious ADD she later admitted to having. She was also very strict with him if he was out of line, and like most people even though she did her best to hide her feelings. Noah could tell if she was getting agitated.

Dianna was also the same age as me I dubbed her the Grandma, because she was softer, and less likely to say No at first. (very valuable skill I learned). She taught me how to be more successful with following through. If you don't say No right away, you yourself have more flexibility to work with. I probably learned the most from Dianna who was very open-minded and just had a natural ability to see through concepts, and get to what really mattered.

It was bound to happen that there would be people that just didn't mix with him. A few were too dry and not animated enough, or were not structured enough. Sometimes it was a combination, where the therapist would have made a great babysitter and maybe was an awesome preschool teacher, but wasn't good at being his therapist.

Logistically though the office itself was not as good as their people. They were not on top of where their people were or if they were going to be late. On day two of the first week of therapy no one showed up for Noah's session. I later found out the office never told the therapist she had to be here. This is probably a sign.

One thing I did learn is when your child has problems with disruptions in routine or is trying to learn one, it's very important your therapists are as committed to the therapy as you and your child. Even if they are at heart committed to the child, this doesn't mean they are committed to the logistics of the job. All parents love their kids, ASD or not, but this doesn't mean they are committed to the recovery road. Or even committed to something in between. Lord knows many of them just want to be committed, I know in my weaker moments I have felt this way.

They used ABA, which is Applied Behavior Analysis, which is very structured and has to do with a child sitting in a chair at a desk touching and working with cards. They also used NET(Natural Environment Teaching) similar to ABA except it is usually on the floor and uses a lot of the toys and items in the environment, but also uses the cards. They did some of the floor time techniques but most of them were not familiar with it.

The behavior therapy is also exactly what it sounds like. The idea of training Noah to regulate himself, work through his anxiety and comply to your request. I read a lot about it, some stories I read the parents swore by it. It was a miracle therapy, but others found it to not really helpful at all and it was too frustrating and anxiety provoking. One thing is for certain; it is one of the very few therapies schools will pay for since it has been backed up by numerous scientific publications. However, I personally watched the entire play starring ABA, and there did come a time when it had to go. But just like all of the therapies out there, it has to be tried to know if it will work or if it won't. No two kids are alike, and neither should be the therapy.

The ups and downs continued his language improved much with a larger vocabulary and better understanding of verb tenses. By September, just nine months into therapy (three with professionals) he is able to construct shabby sentences, Much of which were posed as questions, and much of what he says requires interpretation. " I want more blue." Referring to type of fruit snack. He is now able to communicate some basic needs such as wanting the TV, a certain toy, or drink or even wanting to use the computer. He struggles to learn what is funny, meltdowns are still wonderfully part of a normal day, but the severe ones are about a few times a week, which is less!

All of the therapy began when Noah was four. A year later when he is turning five he goes into the preschool class for disabled kids two or three days a week for about two hours with one of his behavioral therapists. It is a mixed review, and at the end of that summer we decided to do a full year in this program before enrolling Noah into kindergarten. Which was a great blessing, for after I had already agreed to that, I found out kindergarten in Maple Shade is a full day, and I am unaware of what problems will surface the next year. But for now I am just grateful for the people I have found, that seemed to have been sent by the universe because we were thinking about them.

The Big Family Meeting

Breaking the news of Noah's Autism to the family does not go over well as expected. Even before whenever there were questions or concerns they were dismissed. Not necessarily to intentionally pointing blame at us for Noah's "issues". However, knowing what we know, that is what they were saying. I don't blame them, I can understand from their point of view it would be better to think that Noah is just spoiled or lazy or we were then, to accept there is something medically wrong with him. Making it a medical issue adds mystery and takes the power away from them and us from fixing it. This is also probably how many parents feel, and why the news can be so crushing. It's one thing to think you are doing something wrong, since you can change, but when it's out of your control, you may feel helpless. I didn't think about it that way, but I can understand how they did.

We were apprehensive on having a meeting, but it was recommended by all the school staff and his doctors..

Little Squares with Colors

Awareness on what is happening in special needs households is a bit of a greater thing then for other households with babies and toddlers. All new parents struggle with sleep deprivation and the extra cleaning involved that goes with that first year of baby jail. But for us, that year has stretched into four and counting. Noah is nowhere near ready to be potty trained, he is still unaware of when he has to go or is going. He still needs to be fed because he can't hold and navigate utensils very long, he cannot dress himself at all, he does not know how to ask for what he wants more than half the time, and every day is full of teaching, being patient, and dealing with meltdowns. These issues will continue on, some for many years.

But probably the worst part is just how essentially different it is than all of those positive aspects of parenting you always hear about. People will say how wonderful having children is because of all you teach them, all they learn, how they love you unconditionally, and all of the fun that goes into playing with them. But for parents like us, you don't get any of that, you assume your child loves you but if you were to quantify love somehow by making a check list, it would be mostly blank. For our child does not want to play with us, does not show affection, does not look at us often and does not communicate in general. He does not say "I love you", does not say anything to us that wasn't a request for something. My only way to fight any of that is to constantly tell him I love him; knowing how he likes to repeat things, he will eventually just say it, like he repeats "this is jeopardy."

My family is not big on talking about feelings, so there is never a point in sharing any of this with them. I base this on years of experience , such as when your alcoholic mother dies, and typical issues. They understand things like money and bad behavior, but never really how it is beyond our control. I think a lot of people are like this because then they don't feel like they need to help someone if that person, in their mind, should just be doing it themselves. It gets them off the hook.

Minding Manners is willing to hold a family meeting for us, to help explain what Autism is, and how they are helping. And most importantly what the family can do to help Noah. There is much anticipation, I am hoping this will be a breakthrough, maybe they will at least understand if nothing else, how tired we are all the time and why we can't always pick up the phone and call. I am mostly hoping they will somehow be inspired to volunteer their help more, because until something changes dramatically, (such as Noah is suddenly better and no longer has autism or we come into a lot of money to hire help) we are going to need the help. They should always assume we need a break or some groceries, at the basic minimum they should accept we are vulnerable, tired and perhaps they should initiate all contact, most of the time.

We have this meeting in October 2006, Minding Manners has been coming over for about three months now and we are approaching the one-year anniversary of the diagnosis. We have everyone come over around 6 pm that evening hoping to help shed some light on things.

"I guess we should have food-you know how my dad is motivated by his stomach," I lightly joke with Joe.

Joe isn't too amused, and doesn't really feel like feeding anyone; he is right, but I don't even realize this. This is where I make mistakes. For ironically, when I have been in situations such as this, I brought the food. My mistakes are always in this area, I allow too much leniency and do not demand enough of others. It is hard to admit it when you realize that your people are watching you struggle so, perhaps they aren't your friends, or "your people". It's not all their fault, because this is how I said its ok to treat me. For me it's not even a conscious decision to not rock the boat, it comes out as natural as my willingness to help, regardless of what I have going on in the moment.

They pile in and sit around the living room, Grandma and Grand pop, Pop Pop & Nana, Joe's brother, and about four of our close friends. Becky, the director of the company greets them and begins the hour-long chat.

"Thank you all for coming, it means a lot to Joe and Chris to have your support. I want to explain what Autism spectrum disorders are, what you can do to help, and after we can answer questions."

"First of all Autism is a complex developmental disability that causes problems with social interaction and communication. Where children perseverate on objects and experience regular anxiety. This may sound like a lot of medical speak, but most importantly Noah is still Noah, having an ASD or Autism Spectrum Disorder is just one part of him, and really is a label to explain those things that are hard to understand or appear as bad behavior. Typically the symptoms usually start before age three and vary in severity. "

"It is believed with early intervention, the symptoms can be greatly reduced, and with the right type of behavior therapy a child can be mainstreamed into regular classrooms, where they can appear just like any of the other children. None of us have the answers, and no two kids are the same when it comes to symptoms and therapy, what works for one kid may not work on another." She continues on, but now I am thinking, oh great you just told them no one has the answers. I can already tell some of them are starting to be uncomfortable in their seats.

Becky went on to explain how people are never fully prepared for the realities or adjustment to this complex condition. And how each child has to have his or her own individualized program.

"Christine and Joe have the right attitude about making every moment a teaching experience. This of course is exhausting. Noah, also has some social skills, and is not considered severe; he is more in the moderate to high functioning category when we started working with him. We know that Chris and Joe have done a lot of work with Noah; we could tell that right when we started working with him. "She said

And I hoped oh good see, proof, we have a right to be tired.

"Noah is an adorable and bright child; he just doesn't always understand what is being asked of him. He also is more sensitive to certain stimuli: lights are brighter; noise is louder and affects him more than maybe a typical child. Sometimes he will appear hyper because he is bouncing off of furniture or the walls, but this is because he cannot feel where his body is in space. We call this stimming, which is short for Self-Stimulatory behavior and we all do it. Twirling your hair, tapping, fidgeting, even smoking would be considered stims. They are ways of curbing anxiety," Becky explains to the confused crowd

"Is he always going to be this way?" Joe's mom asks

"Currently there is no cure for Autism, but it does not mean he will not be more and more functional." Becky replies

"You should treat him as you would if he did not have a disorder. If he does something bad he still needs to be corrected, he should just be given the opportunity to understand what is being asked of him."

She explains for about an hour, going over the programs they are doing and generally answers the few questions people are brave enough to ask. I don't know if any of this is going to help, but like everything else we have been going through the past ten months, at least we have tried and have done all we can. It was better to have done this than to do nothing.

"Well now I feel bad about nagging you about not calling me enough." One of our friends says to me afterwards.

Within a month he will forget he said this. But he was the only one to this day to ever admit that.

I would like to say this meeting changes things, and everyone gets it and is very supportive, but no. I wish I could say that some were suddenly offering to come over every other day. Maybe even watch Noah occasionally so we can go out and do normal couple stuff. I mostly wish the people I invested in, treated this situation as it should be treated, a serious situation, an emergency. A few brave souls do watch Noah a few times, and Joe's parents help out with some occasional groceries. It would be nice to have more help during the day, so our health didn't have to suffer so much, when that is the last thing that Noah really needs. But for whatever reason, people are busy, people are scared. The Calvary never came, and as a result, life stayed stagnant and disappointing for a long time. I can say there was generally more acceptance of Noah's condition. It will be a couple of years from this point before Noah is ready to spend the night elsewhere, when that does eventually happen some of the stress starts to finally, slowly lift.

My dad realized Noah is at least as stressful as my sister was for him. And Joe's Mom seems to accept it more as truth as opposed to trying to deny it. Most of my friends have not stood by me, my sister reminded me it's because of the company I keep, that I always seem to find the people who need more of my time than I should give. And it is true, I have always had an innate ability to find the lost souls and try to help them, help them help themselves. It started very young with the kid no one else wants to be friends with because she was poor and smelled like pee. But I felt bad for her, and didn't care what other people thought. I suppose this just stuck with me. I have been told by other ASD parents that losing friends is also typical. Some people have lost all of their friends, I am grateful to be blessed with a few very wonderful ones, even if they are scattered around the globe, even though they can't always help in a physical sense I know there are a few out there who have our back.

So this is when you start to find out who your real friends are. And also who is more stable in their life. This is probably true for any parents who have children with special needs. I also think just having kids and aging changes things. Many of my friends were awesome when we were young, as in we had a lot of fun together. But life changes, people marry and move. I don't have any animosity to those friends, for that is just part of the tides of life.

My friend list had changed, some of them were still there, even if they didn't help out as much as we needed. Joes friends though pretty much disappeared, only adding to the isolation he probably already feels. It is not a pleasant time in one's life to discover that you never had solid relationships with your friends right when you need them most. It is also particularly ironic considering the issue at hand has such a huge social component.

All and all, the one thing I can say about having a family meeting is at least, you are certain you have now done and said everything you can to convince those in your life that you need their help. It is now up to them to give it. I would hope for other people who did this that it brought the best out of their friends and family. If not, at least there is the comfort in knowing that since you have such limited time and resources that you do not need to waste it on those who don't appreciate it anyway. You will learn to not ask how they are first, not support them first. For your time is so limited, if you have anything left, it should go to each other, yourself and those who do "get it".

It does give me comfort in knowing I did the best I could, and I accept my people as they are. I have often gone out of my way in the past, and before I was pregnant was more of a doormat. Not a huge one, but I made the mistake of not acknowledging my own needs, and always putting others first. Pregnancy gave me the ability to finally say NO, and once I found I could, I have achieved more balance. I never worry whether someone will be angry with me anymore, especially now; I look at all we have been through and I am rarely angry with them. So if someone was to be angry with me for not doing something, what does that say about them? Are they not paying attention? Sometimes in life it really is our judgments of others that tell us who we are. I learned I am understanding and fair, and have put the needs of others over my own, which is not always ok. I have learned I do not excel at asking for help. I have learned that maybe I didn't think about my own needs when selecting friends.

ACT TWO

Furry Heroes

Noah's Writing Assignment

This story is based on actual events.

I'm having a party.
Fred is only in the party.
At 2:50 am Chewie is bad.
At 3:25 am Chewie is a good dog. So I let Chewie out of my bedroom.
But I let Sami my cat to come to my party.
Now all of my pets come to my party.
At 4:30 all of my pets come back to my bedroom.

Therapy Dog Anyone? Anyone?

Considering that children and therapy are truly like snowflakes, all parents basically go to a Therapy Buffet where you take a little of this and a little of that to figure out which works best. We began thinking about adding a dog just prior to our family meeting in the fall of 2006.

I have always loved dogs and most animals in general, and have had our cat Sami since the day he was born in 1996. He is very tolerant, and has put up with multiple moves, parades of people and animals, and having to adjust to living with now seven different dogs and a few other cats that have either visited from time to time, or were also part of the family.

Sami has always been a great communicator, we have regular conversations, and he makes excellent eye contact, which is something cats are not known for. He has never been on a surface that a human doesn't sit on, he has been a faithful alarm clock, and has often been waiting for me at the door when I get home. Sami has been there for me, and I have always been there for him. He is special; people who do not even like cats love Sami. He has often been a compass to determine how positive a person is-if Sami doesn't like you, there is usually a good reason. He is massively afraid of the vacuum cleaner, as is Noah. But Sami is unaffected by thunderstorms or rain. He is fully trained and has awesome manners and a personality to boot. I figure if I can train a cat, then a dog would be easier. Sami is a friendly cat, but he is still a cat and is not a durable as a dog. As I was looking into it, I discovered there are service dogs for kids with Autism.

"Hey, Joe, look at this, we can get a puppy trained just for Noah to be a service dog for him." I say excitedly while looking at the computer one of many nights doing research.

"What would it do? "

"Besides eat, sleep, poop and love you?" I joke. This reminded myself of something my well-meaning Grand mom said when I first had Noah. We finally knew he was a boy; my grandmother seemed relieved, saying, "What are you going to do with a girl?"

I remember thinking, "Love it?"

I read to Joe:" It says here they help with anxiety, can be trained to lap the child to keep the child from hurting itself, they can alert you if the child is wandering at night or trying to escape the house, and even can help with socialization. Not to mention the stress relief it could give us" I was uber excited

"Can they train it to clean up after itself?" Joe always has a dry sarcastic sense of humor, but he will not burst my bubble.

As I was looking into the request help area a big rock burst my bubble.

"It says here the waiting list is two years. That can't be right, these kids need help yesterday not two years from now! Maybe I should check another company." I then look into other companies and it was more of the same varying from 18 months to three years of waiting. Frankly, all you do is wait when it comes to ASD, but in no way was I willing to do this. I understand it takes time to fully train the dog, but since it's a personalized thing, the dog would be with us during that time. All of the programs preached of how they select the dog for the child and it's specially trained. This is also why it cost between 6,000-10,000 dollars. Which I would find a way to get, but not if I still had to wait two or more years for the dog. The waiting list was not the training period; it is the time it took to begin the process.

So not being one to be a big gloomy Gus, I try to think how I can achieve this without having to wait besides writing a million letters, which I 'm known to do. I decide to do some research on therapy dogs, and ask other people if they had worked with any, and where the parents got them.

The next day when Dianna was here for Noah's session I jump right to it after some quick hellos.

"Do any of your clients use therapy dogs, or have you?"

"Actually, Becky has a border collie that is a therapy dog; I can ask her where she got him."

"That would be helpful. I am having a difficult time trying to get this going where it's not going to take years to happen, and holding a fundraiser may be fun but not really something I have time to organize."

"Oh a doggie, that would be a nice addition, I know Becky's dog really does help keep everyone just a bit more regulated."

"I think it would be the next step in friendship too, first plush animals, then the real thing, maybe then he will want to make friends with people." I said

"Well we won't know until we try."

The next part is figuring out which breeds would be the best candidates for such a job and start applying to shelters and rescue centers for puppies. Part of the therapy I had learned was to have the dog and child grow up together. I knew Border Collies are suitable, but I was sure there were others too. Border Collies are really intelligent dogs, I've even seen one trained to read.

First of all, any breed can be a therapy dog; it really depends on the dog. You are mostly looking for a confident dog, not one that is dominant or passive, one that doesn't require a lot of grooming, Larger dogs are usually better then smaller dogs because they can do more, but are harder to put under a table in restaurants, and one that is more people-oriented than environment oriented. Which is why field dogs aren't normally used, nor are fancy breeds like Shih Tzus.

There is no national formal certification required for therapy dogs, but a lot of places prefer you have a certificate from the American Kennel Club for what is called a Canine Good Citizen Award. It is basically ten tests given to the dog and handler, mostly having to do with manners, calm and pleasant personality, and being well groomed. This award is normally a gateway to other AKC programs, and is more a reward for good behavior than anything else. I did not know there were no formal laws for service dogs. In fact if you train your own dog, it is up to you whether or not you have them registered as such, or whether you carry any ID. However, to avoid problems its best to have a harness or ID badge with your dog's name and photo. All of that can be done on the Internet. And it's covered by the Americans with

Disabilities Act and can be found in the United States Government web pages.

So after a lot of research it looks like we are looking for a medium to large size dog with a good temperament, that is highly trainable and intelligent and preferably one that is bred to have a soft mouth, since any dog can bite, (well as long as they have teeth). I am partial to Shadow, the Golden retriever from the movie *Homeward Bound*, (he was my dog hero). And to narrow the overwhelming field of possibilities I decide to look for one of them, while keeping the Border collie or Labrador in the back of my mind also.

I did not anticipate such a long process to adopt a dog. Shelters are so crowded their residents sometimes have to be euthanized, you would think there'd be an eagerness to get them adopted. Preferably in the right homes, so why the long wait? Interview the family and get them their dog. But no, we are on lists and lists and wait months again to hear from someone. I want to adopt over buying mostly because of the expense. Pet store dogs are still dogs regardless of the owner making money off of them; they need loving homes and get euthanized also when they get to old to be sellable. But they come at a much larger price tag, where at a shelter it might be 150-200 dollars. This is before I ever heard of puppy mills. So one day, after being tired of waiting (again) I just go to the local pet shop and buy a puppy.

Fred went to Hollywood

I was bringing the items into the house from my latest grocery trip when Joe popped out of the garage to help.

"Can you get the rest of it from the back seat?" I ask and wait as he went to the back seat to find a furry little friend.

"Really?" he exclaimed like a 7-year-old boy

"Well, I had been seeing this little guy at that new pet shop up town and decided I don't feel like waiting much anymore, and he was on sale.

There is a new pet shop in our small town that had the nicest little wooden pens where they kept the puppies. Much better than cages, the dogs had room to play and seemed happy. It smelled like cedar chips in there and the people running it were dog groomers who love dogs. It seemed like a nice place to get our puppy, since we have had no luck adopting. Plus I like to keep our money in town whenever possible.

"They had both a male and a female, but this guy seemed much more calm then the other one. He would grab his toy and sit there with it in his mouth, tail a-wagging." I said proudly

Joe carries the 12-week-old Golden Retriever in the house so we can show him around. I had already purchased books, had puppy proofed months ago, and now it was time to show him to Noah.

Noah has had an interest in animals and especially dogs for some time, but he is four and a half, and ASD or no ASD, it's still an age where they have to be taught how to handle a puppy.

Noah approaches the dog in a curious fashion; I nearly expect them to sniff each other's butts since Noah is a man of few words.

"Can we name him Fred?" I ask now sounding like a 7-year-old. "I always wanted to name my last childhood dog Fred or Ralph but my dad said they were stupid names." (So we named that dog Fluffy instead.)

"What do you think Noah?" Joe asked

"Fred's okay" Noah said

And off, run boy and dog through the house, Noah really seems to like that the dog is his size, not realizing how big Fred was going to be. Goldens grow to about 75 pounds and about 22 inches tall; they are a lot of dog. But for the next few months, he will be small.

House training goes easily Fred is a natural, we take him out on a schedule and he has very few if any accidents in the house. (Wish I could say the same for Noah who is still in diapers at this point.) We crate him at night, and after the first few nights he adjusts and is not whining. He seems to like his little den, and is a "good egg".

Noah learns to play with Fred with Fred's toys, but mostly Fred just follows Noah around. The only problem is the dog sometimes humps, but he was so young I don't think it is really the same thing. So every now and then Noah repeats me by saying "No Humping" At least he is learning new words.

I spend time during the day teaching Fred to sit and lay down, and am really impressed with how quickly he learns everything. And am very optimistic about the future - I see how much he is bringing Noah out of his shell already. Fred isn't much of an eater; he takes frequent breaks to nibble at his food but barely eats the bowls worth. So he and Noah have that in common also.

Fred doesn't bark but has this cute little purring sound he makes like a cat, but since he is a dog it is even cuter. I probably should have taken that as a sign.

However, due to stress and fatigue we miss that poor Fred is incubating an illness. Three weeks after we get him we had to rush him to the vet at night because he is panting and couldn't seem to breathe well.

The vet does all they can for the low price of $1200, but does not save him; sadly he dies the next morning. I am very sad; it is the last straw and not being a crier, (well anymore), I find myself in tears the whole morning and into the next month. All that potential, just gone, my only comfort is knowing we gave him a loving home for three whole weeks. Noah picks up on my sadness and is also sad, he doesn't know what happened to Fred, and finally asks where he is.

So I tell him a lie like most parents do in these situations, death is not something young children understand, especially kids who do not get the world exists beyond their minds. So I say Fred is going to be a Big Star and moved to Hollywood. He has since starred in many *Air Bud* movies and sends Noah a Christmas present the following two Christmas's. The first being a few weeks away and we do not even have a tree, let alone much in the way of gifts. Ironically the dog was considered an early gift. With all the money that went out to save the house, save the dog, and pay for therapies, there is less than nothing left.

One day shortly thereafter I must have felt like torturing myself and go to PetSmart when it is having an animal adoption day. I speak to one of the groups there who refer me to a woman from an advocacy group that works for helping educate people about puppy mills, and helps with consumers who have unknowingly purchased sick puppies. I have never heard of puppy mills before this. Apparently they are" mass production "breeders not interested in the breeds as much as the dollars involved, who separate puppies from their mothers too early to move them faster for a quicker turnaround but the puppies do not have all of their mother's immunities. Then the puppies are shipped on trucks with so many other puppies that illnesses can be passed very easily, and sometimes silently.

In our case, Fred incubated a form of pneumonia and because Golden Retrievers are so interested in keeping you happy, he did not complain. The purring was a sign, as was the fact he nibbled at his food.

Fortunately this nice woman is willing to help us file a complaint with a consumer rights organization of NJ. We do get back the money we paid for the dog, (thanks to Visa), and I am also lucky that I know the person from the Board of Health that investigates the puppy shop. They find the local shop also has many other sick dogs because of those nice cedar and wood pens the puppies are in.

The shop is clean, but apparently you cannot keep animals in wood pens because of disease. The shop is shut down and out of the puppy business. At least Fred helped save other kids from this trauma, and his death was not in vain, and I am grateful he died before Christmas, because the only thing that would have been any sadder would have been to wake up on Christmas morning to a dead dog.

If only I could Have a Puppy, I'd call Myself so Very Lucky....

After the trauma of Fred subsides, I decide to be more optimistic and start saving money in a glass jar for a new dog. I decorate it with pictures of puppies, and Noah and I played the Puppy Song by Harry Nilsson almost daily. I keep following up with shelters and rescue groups, looking in the paper, and decided that one day the right dog will just wander up to our porch.

In March, I find a site on the Internet called *Puppy Finder*; it basically has puppies from shelters, rescue centers, and reputable breeders and gives you contact information so you can request to see a certain new friend to find out if you are compatible. One day there is an ad for some puppies that were about to be old enough to go to new homes, they were born on an Amish farm in Lancaster Pa, which is about 75 miles away.

I call the ad placer who represented the breeder and make an appointment to go out there that Saturday to meet the puppies. I remind Joe it was to look, and not necessarily buy. I had saved a few hundred dollars at this point, and the puppies were being sold about 100.00 more than the local shelters, not the 800 dollars I paid for poor defective Fred. So it was a possibility, our friends Meghan and Nick agree to drive us out there with Noah to see the dogs. Meghan was interested in getting a puppy too, but her mother was reluctant because of their older dog. She hadn't fully decided either way, and I think Meghan hopes that once she saw a puppy, if she got one that is, her mom would just fall in love and all would be right in the world.

The drive out to Lancaster is exciting, so much so for Noah he throws up all over Nick's backseat. We stop at a local strip mall to clean him up and get a new shirt.

We arrive at the farm at dusk and the sun is setting and making the sky a beautiful shade of orange. A young girl in Amish dress showed us to the puppies that are being kept in a typical wire pen, not as pretty as the store, but I already felt better about that. I put my hand in the pen and 5 puppies are immediately licking my arm, there is no way we are leaving empty handed.

"Aw, I want that one." Meghan exclaims pointing to one of the puppies that had dirt on its nose, who proceeded to then puppy bite her finger.

Joe and I held two different ones, performing the puppy test. You basically put the puppy on its back and see if it's comfortable being that way, this shows it's more passive then aggressive. Then you put it down and step away from it and see if it follows you.

"two for two so far." Joe said all smitten, that tough guy.

The remainder of the test is basically touching the dog, gently tugging on its ears and paws to see if it is going to growl or exhibit dominance. The puppies passed all of this with flying colors. We checked out the mom and dad on the premise, the mom seemed to know what was up and was barking a bit at the people handling her babies. They were both beautiful Goldens and were from champion AKC blood lines, very gentle and friendly despite the fact she knows we are there to take at least one of her offspring. But I assure her; he is going to a good home and will be very loved.

Meghan decides she is leaving with one also, we make the decision in the car on the way back that hers can stay at our house for a little while why she prepares her home and her mom. Her puppy nibbles on everything in sight (I don't think she did the puppy test) and changes his name from Marley to Chewie.

" Noah, what do you want to name our new friend here?" I ask him

" Lets name him Fred." Noah said rather matter-of-factly. I should have guessed this is the same kid that has to have the same sneakers every year.

" Fred it is then."

After this whenever we had to refer to our first Fred we would call him Original Fred, and eventually O.F for short.

Fred and Chewie are all nestled in their crate quite comfortably and barely make a sound overnight. They both have great appetites and would woof down a bowl of food three times a day.

" Poor O.F, he really was sick, I can't believe they just ate those busy bones in fifteen minutes, it would take O.F two days to get through it."

Meghan and Nick come over every day to help with the puppy care and bonding, after the first week I begin to wonder if "mom" was going to release her foot, or is it permanently down.

" I am sure once she meets Chewie she will love him." I assure Meghan who doesn't seem too sure about it. " It might be a good thing for Dolly to have a puppy to pester her."

Dolly is some ridiculously old unknown age; she just keeps living and has no problem barking at people, cars, and motorcycles.

" I really don't want this to be another burden for you. " Meghan says to me with some worry.

" As long as you're paying for his food and what not, what's the difference if there is one or two? They love each other's company, and they will be life-long friends. So far it is not a big deal." I reassure her

About two months later though, they came over to care for Chewie less and less, and seem more distant to him. I think back to one night when our friends Keith and Kevin were visiting right after we brought them home.

" I hope you know you're going to have two dogs." Kevin said in a rather chipper voice and with much conviction

My thought back then, was that he was being silly, but it turns out he was right. Meghan never takes on her Mother about the dog, and though she was willing to find him another home, I don't feel it's appropriate. He has been here this long, I have nursed him through one illness already, and Fred and Noah are really attached to him. As was I, but Joe on the other hand often jokes with people that because they are the hundredth visitor they win a dog. Part of me felt like he needs to stay since he is not a piece of furniture that she just doesn't have room for. Besides, what was the difference if we have one or two, it was just twice the love. It was twice the poop to clean up, but the yard needs to be cleaned anyway. Joe wasn't completely convinced but eventually realizes Chewie isn't going anywhere.

" If I wanted two dogs, we would of bought two dogs". Joe grumbles.

" Well then think of Chewie as a toy for Fred that keeps Fred in line. Or that we are keeping him for parts." I joke

" I hope you realize they will just be house dogs, we won't be able to train Fred to be a therapy dog like we hoped."

I don't believe this fully and figure I can make the time to train them both. I haven't yet realized that Chewie will be more of a challenge then I think.

That Dog's not Right.

Fred and Chewie are growing up nicely, it's amazing how different they are from poor O.F, who just completed work on Air Buddies, we are very proud. They are eating machines, and they love to play and lick you. The training is going well, and they both successfully learned to sit, stay, come, lay down by the time they are six or seven months old.

Chewie learned how to speak, but that eventually became something I wished I didn't teach him.

" Chewie, how do you spell DOG?" I ask

Chewie barks back three times, and I say the letters along as he barks and then praise him after the G. It is a cute parlor trick, and he is so enthusiastic about his talent, he sometimes barks like that when people come in.

I also begin to notice the differences between Fred and Chewie. Fred is a bit more laid back and usually takes his commands regardless of what is going on around him. Chewie can be called to come in, but if a butterfly flies by he will go chase it, but Fred will still come in.

Chewie regularly sits in the back yard staring at the trees and you would think he is deaf because you have to call him louder and louder. Something about this is oddly familiar.

" I think Chewie has some form of doggie ADHD." I say one night to Joe

"Well that would explain a lot, That dog's not right." Joe replies in his best Hank Hill impersonation.

Their body types are different also, Fred is your standard golden and is shaped like a little tank, and now a big one, where Chewie is more elongated and lean, and has a really narrow head. But this also makes him more aerodynamic, he can beat Fred in any foot race. Chewie however is more nervous than Fred, when he was a puppy as soon as it got dark he would be more jumpy and cowardly, where Fred is non-reactive. If you didn't know they came from the same litter, where raised the same way, and ate the same food, you would think they belonged to different people. But regardless of their differences, they are like peas and carrots they just love each other.

People joke with me that we aren't feeding Chewie, but he eats just as much as Fred, in fact after a while I intentionally fed him more, this has done nothing to change his appearance. I point this out to my friends who complain about their weight.

" See he eats more than Fred, and the same stuff, and is no more active than Fred yet he is slimmer. But Fred is the one that is actually normal."

Chewie can't help what he looks like or who he is, any more than any of us can help it.

Rising above your fear is a difficult task for anyone, and having to realize something like weight control is also related to genetics takes a person's control away

Even though we didn't expect Chewie, or intended on having him, he is mostly big fun. He likes to dance with you; and is very tolerant and never grumpy. He loves food and licking people, he plays ball better than Fred. They both will go out to retrieve the ball I throw, but only Chewie brings it back when outside. Fred just runs along and makes it look good, but never brings it back. As if he is just saying to you, 'There it is!". The weird thing is, Fred will play fetch in the house, often just bringing me a toy to throw regardless of how tired I am. Chewie never initiates any play. More similarities to Noah, I am beginning to wonder if Chewie is a doggie version of Noah, and if he becomes a handful, well you can always find him a new home, which can't be said of Noah. But would I really want to?

There is a loud crash radiating in the Florida room, I hurry myself out there to find both dogs somehow in the yard, staring at the house.

" How did you guys get out here? I ask them waiting for them to answer me. I noticed the back door is still locked. Then I notice the glass, and realize at least one of the them jumped through the window to break it, and the other must of followed.

After the shock wears off all I could say is " Bad! Bad Dogs." And rushed them back in so I can clean up the glass.

" You could have been really hurt! Wait until Daddy gets home." more yelling at them, they just look back with doggie smiles because they don't understand English yet.

I clean up the glass and tack up a sheet over the broken window. This is the first of two windows they have broken, but besides that, they never ruin anything else.

"Well boys. " I say to them as they look at me with those puppy dog eyes

" Looks like we really need to figure out how to get you two to stop jumping, or else its snip snip" I say and I swear a look of worry went over Fred face as if he knew I was referring to his balls and being neutered.

I am holding off on the neutering since I do want to show Fred in dog shows, we thought it would be a great thing for Noah to do since both boy and dog would have a routine to follow, and have to display that they can follow directions as a unit. But he has to wait until he is 10. I don't think it is fair or wise to neuter Chewie while Fred got to keep his. Chewie already has a complex; I don't want to add to it.

The dogs have definitely brought a lot out of Noah. He is laughing more, and talking to the dogs. We teach Noah how to do a lot of the commands with the dogs, and how to play with them. Plus they do exactly what I expect them too. They alert us at night when Noah is out of his room with their Noah bark, they help with calming down to all of to us and to Noah by just petting them. Just looking at them often makes me smile and laugh, and I think they feel that way looking at us.

Later on in the day when they are out of the doghouse and back in the real house life gets suddenly better for them. Noah is back home and they both went running to give him lots of kisses. Which, Noah does not always appreciate.

"I want to play with Fred ONLY." Noah bluntly states, stretching out the word only, to show his sincerity.

Noah and Fred were playing a game of chase that ended with Fred jumping up on Noah's bed and making himself comfortable. Fred often likes to happily lay on Noah's bed since Noah's room is often full of plush toys. And Plush toys are Fred's weakness-he is addicted to them often stealing them from Noah's room.

Sometimes it is necessary to separate the drooling duo- not only does Noah need it to be this way, it's good for them as well. So I let boy and Fred run off and put the baby gate up to keep Chewie in the living room with me. Which he was okay with for the most part, only when I left the room did he seem upset, not that I blame him. But as long as he can see me he is fine and is lying there waiting his turn. I know how hard it is for him to focus and listen and how much harder he has to work than Fred. Which is why even though he can be annoying, I doubt we would ever find him a new home.

One day I do hope to take Chewie to one of those obedience trials that Fred can Ace, for even though he takes longer to sit, and is deaf sometimes when I call him. I know he can do it, he has his moments where he does listen just fine but it has a lot to do with him not getting distracted. So his victory will be all the greater when he does succeed. I have this image in my mind that one day when Noah is old enough both he and Chewie will be in that ring, Boy and dog with their quirks, and attention problems. And they will do it; they will complete all the trials, and get their little trophy, which Noah would really love. Their victory, proving that even the distracted can focus; they just have to work harder. I see it so clearly, Noah and Chewie doing a lap around the ring and Chewie licking Noah in the face and Noah not minding.

What Does Not Kill Us Makes Us Crazy

Playing in the backyard should be a relaxing and fun time. We consider ourselves fortunate to have a backyard and that we do not live in a city or an apartment complex where the backyards are just unused parking lots that are draped with concrete rather than grass and dirt. However, as long as a child doesn't have access to a jackhammer, they generally cannot throw the contents of a concrete backyard.

My husband Joe and I were sitting in the enclosed porch that is fancifully called a Florida room, sharing details of our day while Noah was playing in the yard with Fred and Chewie. Suddenly I notice Noah throwing dirt and sticks over the fence into our neighbors yard, something he has been told many times not to do, and when he has continued to do so, he has to come in immediately and cut play time short. This generally does not go over well at all and always results in a huge tantrum, full of flailing and screaming. And Noah is always very upset as well.

"Hey Noah, we don't throw things over the fence, remember? If you have to throw stuff, just throw it on your slide. The Slide is Ok," I tell him very matter-of-factly.

He gives me that blank stare and says nothing; I know I am in trouble now. How I wish he could read me as well, maybe that would avoid the whole series of events that is about to unravel.

Noah now comes over to the house and starts throwing rocks at it and the dogs. The dogs fortunately are not fazed, they have been taught to be very tolerant of Noah and his erratic and unpredictable behavior. I remind Joe of this when he is feeling down about his parenting skills; "See we taught the dogs, it's not you, it's him.

Here comes the second warning.
"Come on Noah, what did I just say?" More nothing from his end. "If you throw stuff again, and it's not on your slide you have to come inside. Do you just want to come in?"

He approaches rather abruptly with more stares, his fists are shaking with unearthed dirt and grass ready to toss it in my general direction. I remind him not to do it or he will have to go in. I take a step towards him so he knows I am serious.
"No I want to stay outside!" he finally yells

"Then play the right way and it's all Ok," I calmly tell him while I still am calm. I know I give him these opportunities because I want him to learn to calm himself down, and to not make it a bigger deal. Right now, all he did was make a mistake and did something he should not have done. Right now he has a chance to not make a bigger one, and continue with his playtime. I am giving him a choice; I am telling him what is going to happen. But really all I am giving him is more rope.

Blank look is still there as he throws the dirt and rock pile at the house. Now the chase begins. As soon as he does it I go to bring him in, remind him what he did that was wrong and what he could have done instead. But he is running from me and screaming. "No I can't go in! I can't go in!"

I catch him and bring him into his room where the real fun begins. Now he is grabbing hold of the doorway to prevent the inevitable, kicking and screaming the whole way. I know I have to put him down and basically hurdle over things and get to the door first otherwise this same scenario will continue to play over and over, like some autism version of hell. After a few minutes of this, and finally getting to the door first I remind him he has to be in there for six minutes to calm down one minute for every year he is old and I admit I too would like to be put in a time-out sometimes (at this point I would be able to go sit in my room for thirty-four minutes, and that would be just fine with me).

If he does calm down and apologize all will be well; if he does not, he loses his new best friend Power, a Webkinz JR. That is the one thing he is attached to at the moment. Autistic kids do not have the same "currency" as typical ones, for a long while, Noah had no attachments, and nothing he held of value. It's very difficult to get your child to comply when there is nothing you can use as currency, or as punishment. But for now, there is Power, and he does not want to lose his new Thunderstorm protection buddy.

Noah does calm down for the most part; he apologizes and we then go out front to wait for Grandma and Grandpa who are picking him up for the weekend. He is excited and happy about going over there, and even has a birthday party to attend on Saturday. Due to traffic, Grandma and Grandpa are about a half hour late and as soon as Noah sees them he states rather loudly "I can't go with you". This on one hand is unexpected since we have been prepping him all week, and even just a few hours before, heck, even just an hour before it was a great idea. But, they were late, so now the whole thing is messed up. We redirect him several times and do silly things to make him get off the track of "I can't go with you." Eventually he found some relaxation playing with the water hose, and this was fine until he could not stop squirting us, even after being told multiple times to stop. He kept going for the hose when it was taken away, and I had to physically carry him in the house and repeat the same scenario as before with his room.

Now the stakes are higher, and if he does not comply I am going to take away the beloved Webkinz Jr. Power. He does not comply, he does not calm down, he does not get his pet. He does however still get put in the car about ten minutes later to go to Grandma and Grandpa's because in no way was that going to fall through. This was the ugliest of all, he has to be restrained in his car seat, which he gets out of and opens the door of a running, but not yet moving car (they should have had his door locked, but unfortunately in these times, perfection even from adults cannot be expected). Now he is screaming he can't go with them. 'No I can't go with you!! Over and over he screams this, louder and louder, that he needs kisses, and eventually his words and screams just turn to high pitch shrills as they drive away with Grandpa having to hold him down in his seat. Grandma was probably glad for the first time she lost most of her hearing.

I know it's not his fault, and for him the anxiety, the terror is real. But so is my stress level right now all of the logic in the world does not curb the need for flight or fight when you are already there. Sure, it can help you process it later; it can even help you rationalize certain fears beforehand.

Overcoming a fear of spiders or cats can be taught with enough logic and repetition, as well as avoidance. But too much input, too much noise is just overwhelming after a while, leaving the person full of anxiety, not because they are afraid of noise, not because they even are in fear of anything at the moment.

Yet, the body does not react as such; the body wants it to stop. Run or fight! And when it's your child that is causing this, you know neither choice is the solution, hence compounding the problem. You can't very well just go for a walk or a run and leave your child alone, and you can't fight with your child because that only makes the situation worse. The only comfort you can find is now you know what it is like for them during any normal day. Any given day, they can feel as you do right now, it may not be a very strong feeling constantly, it may not have bubbled over yet. But the pot is always simmering, always ready to boil over if the heat is just turned up a little. What is truly remarkable is how well they can keep it together for so many hours a day.

I have lived with Noah having multiple tantrums a day total time spent could be three to four hours out of the day, and it eventually decreased to maybe half this, then maybe to where it wasn't every single day. And when you are under stress, and you know that the other ten hours aren't filled with it, does not matter. You do not feel grateful in that moment, even if logically you should.

But you do not feel it. I can't help but notice, how that is probably how the child feels as well. He may be grateful to everyone during those other times and even to himself for holding it together, but, when that pot boils over, does it matter? It's still boiled over, and it always will it will depend on who is turning up the heat and how often they do it. The water does not control the burner-the burner controls the water. So expecting it to all go away or be trained away is ridiculous. No, the only way for water not to boil when heat is being applied that cannot be turned off is to add ice to the water, consistently.

"I guess I should have just let him play with the hose," I said to Joe, now beaten down after the whole incident.

"Well you couldn't let him do that, then you're not following through," he replied frustrated as well.

"Yeah, well I follow through all the time, and if consistency is what works, then how come it's not working? No, maybe sometimes, when his cork is about to pop, I should switch gears and tell him I have changed my mind."

I don't think Joe fully wanted to accept that, he still is having issues on his own parenting skills, and I admit the thought didn't cross my mind at the time because his mom was right there. Some part of me was still insecure about what she would think of me by not following through.

I know how far his parents have come now, but they are still floating down the denial river. They would much rather believe we cause all this. So we being very consistent proves that is wrong. But it isn't helping Noah, or anyone else.

About an hour later Grand Pop called to let us know they arrived safely. Which was of concern; I know how difficult it can be to drive with him in the car having a full-blown meltdown. They said he calmed down about 15 minutes into the drive, which is a win actually. They put Noah on the phone so he could tell us himself.

"Hey buddy, how are you feeling?" I asked

"I'm doing fine, we are going to go see Ralph" Noah said rather calmly as if nothing happened.

Grand pop has a lot of eclectic garden and yard decorations and Ralph is half a mannequin dressed in a sweatshirt and hat that sits at the outside table, Grand-pop's version of a scarecrow that keeps noisy neighbors away. I would like to say that Noah named Ralph, but no it was actually Grand pop.

Even though there are kids next door, Noah still prefers adults and Ralph mostly because they are both more predictable than kids. And, well, as realistic as Ralph may be, he still doesn't say much, which I think suits both Noah and Grand pop just fine.

"Okay, well, have fun we will see you Sunday." I told him.

"Okay see you Sunday"

That was it; the big ridiculous event is now a thing in the past, and one of hundreds we have gotten through. I would like to say it has gotten easier, but really when your child is hysterical and thrashing about there is no getting used to it; I would imagine it only would be if you felt nothing. And feeling nothing may seem like a great idea at the time it isn't. Struggle is often nature's way of strengthening and I think of this when times get tough. Each event actually helps prepare you and makes you more tolerant in other areas of your life. Things that may normally bother a person, or use to bother me do not get under my skin so easily.

Still, sometimes when we are in the heat of battle, the idea of being washed in nothingness is appealing because it's a relief of it all at the moment. But it is not what I would prefer because I have felt that feeling before. And it is not as if you can choose to feel nothing only when times are bad that feeling carries over and steals all of your joy as well. I at least am grateful that I know I will get through the time and in the back of my mind I am still okay with it all.

Bad Behavior

If someone were to walk into another person's home and see a child in a full blown tantrum, kicking, screaming and flailing about on the floor, they would likely assume something was taken away from the child, whether it is a toy or a privilege. This is the scene that Dianna, one of our main behavior therapists walks into one morning. Dianna has worked with us for over a year with Noah, she is the "nice soft grandma type". She is always cheerful, patient and best of all very open minded to trying different therapies. I have felt very comfortable with her from the beginning, she gets my out-of- the-box thinking and we make an excellent team for Noah.

" What happened?" she asks as she turns the corner hearing and then seeing the commotion

" I was reheating my coffee in the microwave and foolishly hit the start button before he was in here to see it." I explain as Noah was practically biting my leg like an angry dog

This is one of the major differences in households with children with ASD, sure we have a lot of your typical issues with our kids on what they can or can't do, and then there are these situations you in no way can possibly see coming, at least not until they have happened more than once.

It is safe to assume the session is not going to start on time; however, the learning has already begun. Now is an opportunity to try to redirect Noah, and calm his anxiety over what to us is a ridiculous issue. But for Noah, the fear is real-who knows what he tells himself. In his mind, missing the timer could be a sign of things going wrong. Whatever it is, the intensity is real, even if it doesn't make logical sense.

So Dianna works her magic finding something to redirect him by offering him something he would highly want to do. This way his attention is being put on something he wants, if you can get him focused on that for long enough, the need for being upset will pass. The trick is to offer him something he likes that is also a calming activity, like playing with water.

Dianna lures him to the bathroom with water balloons; Noah plays with these long enough to forget all about the incident with the microwave. The timing here is good-she entered when the meltdown had only just begun, the level of anxiety was reaching critical mass, but it was able to be diverted.

I hear the tone of his voice change and he becomes more relaxed.

" All better."

Bad behavior goes hand in hand with anxiety, and frustration, especially when the child does not understand you. And there are many levels of not understanding, they may not know some of the words you are using, or don't hear them in the proper context. There are also the times, they don't hear you at all, and you can't understand why they are suddenly flipping out.

Before we had any therapists and I was working with Noah for those seven or eight months, the first thing I learned from other Mom's stories was to make him ask for everything before I give it to him. It would be frustrating but he would learn.

"Noah do you want a cookie?" I ask him knowing of course he would, what I really want is to hear him answer me.

Nothing, just blankness, as if he is deaf or I am not speaking. He just sits in his chair staring off at the TV; Sponge Bob is flipping crabby patties, again. I repeat myself, and eventually wave my hand in front of his face. He responds
"Cookie"

This does not mean he actually wants the cookie, he just repeated the last thing he heard. This happens on a regular basis when he hears me say things to him.

So I ask him again, differently " Say I want a cookie please"

He comes out of his world long enough to say this statement. I am only able to get him to say this because I first use the one thing that matters to him: The remote control to the TV

It all begins with this statement. " I want the remote please" that's it; I wanted him to say those five words together instead of " mote, or Remote". I would not give it to him until he said it correctly.

The first time and several after are frustrating but it doesn't stay there. I repeat " Say I want the remote please" he first says " remote please" No, Noah say " I want the remote please"...he is not paying attention then repeats the last part again, remote please". The third time I break it down, with him copying each word in the sentence. Say "I"- "want"," the remote" "please". He did this! I praise him and repeat it a 4th or 5th time all as one, and he gets it. Then I hand him the remote.

It's not like he gets it for good; ASD kids' victories are often brief and bittersweet. I replay this same scenario several dozen times over a month or two.

But he does eventually start doing it on his own, and now that I have something to build on. I get him to ask for everything this way, substituting remote for whatever the item is.

This is why I believe Autism is often a test of patience and tolerance for the rest of us. We have to push beyond our normal limits of common sense, and give into the idea of the definition of insanity. Which Einstein describes as doing the same task over again, but expecting a different outcome. So I guess we are all crazy if we are doing it right.

Another area of communication is asking him about something he wants to do. Before there was a diagnosis even, there was the issue of what movie he wanted. He was not really into playing things with me, but he loved watching movies.

" Do you want to watch Pooh? " I ask hoping to get a real response like a Yes! But no, he stares blankly off at the TV, though it looks like he isn't even seeing it. I repeat the question, waving my hand in front of his face and he eventually responds.

"Pooh"

I go to put on Pooh and he has a huge flip out screaming, jumping flailing about just because it's what he said, it's not what he meant. Whatever he was watching I guess was fine (though I think it was just the news bulletin on channel 19, the local community channel).

Back before therapy, before dogs, before diagnosis, Noah has maybe twenty words ; most of them are food related. He repeats back things you say, so hearing *cookie* or *Pooh* when asking a question is at least a response you know he can hear. But that doesn't mean that's what he wanted to say or even that he understands the question. For I have given him a cookie, and he has also flipped out..

Sometimes when Noah blanks out and is somewhere else, unable to hear what I am saying. I switch gears and say, " This is Jeopardy!" that gets his attention, it looks strange to an outsider, but I eventually learn not to care about that.

Besides teaching how to ask for things I find it important to try to relate to him-go into his world so he would come into mine which was why I felt Floor-time is such a valid tool. I know if there is a heaven Stanley Greenspan already has preferred parking there, at least I hope so.

Noah is still very particular about things, but flexibility has to be taught, and it's an important skill. Truly when Darwin was talking about survival of the fittest, what he meant was "he who is most adaptable", and adaptable is something Noah is attempting to learn.

One time I was giving him yogurt for breakfast as he previously agreed too, and when I give it to him with the spoon in it, he flips out. Because I guess he was not expecting the spoon to already be there, same kind of thing happens when cutting a banana that he wants to be whole. He is known to throw the food, scream, yell, hit himself in the head or hit me, throw things at me, kick and carry on for nearly an hour over, what seems like minor offenses, but are huge to him. These times were definitely full of stress, and stress is no fun, no fun at all.

Where did he go now?

I wonder from time to time if ABA could be contributing to the problem of Obsession. Children are trained that if there is a request made of them and they can't or don't want to complete it, they are continued to be pressured to do so. Most of the time this turns into an upsetting experience for everyone, with a large tantrum ensuing. After the child calms down they are required to come back to the very thing that upset them to begin with, even if they are still stressed, just managing better.

This is a Catch-22, because what this is intending to teach is to obey. The therapist is going to make them continue and go through with the task because the patient was asked to do it. However it also teaches them if you don't get what you want, just keep pushing and then you get it. Since, that is the result for the therapist. This is both good and bad. Persistence in life often helps a person achieve a goal, get a better job, finish school, and many other positive things. It also is what leads a child to frustration when they are not given what they want, and is what will make them continue to ask. If not for being persistent all children would be "well behaved", in the fact they would not continue to try to do something they are told not to do.

I have seen this happen over and over, where Noah gets stuck on something that he wants to happen a certain way, he will continue to expect it to happen that way, and will not be able to let it go. This is not his life every second of the day, fortunately. It is something that seems to coincide with anxiety. Noah generally does not generalize, each instance and experience is a brand new one. If he has to hold your hand in the parking lot, but he was taught this at Target, he has to be taught it everywhere. Because Target is one place each new place is just that.

One afternoon when we are actually free from therapy because someone couldn't make it, I decide to take Noah out to Target to pick up a few things. I know I have a forty-five minute window, and he is allowed to pick out one toy for ten dollars as reward for working hard, and to keep him motivated.

The next hour I spend trying to get him ready to go. This includes the abnormal amount of time it takes to get him dressed because he can't stay still and falls down a lot while dressing him, and for the period of time he keeps wandering the yard. Then suddenly he wants to ride in the front seat.

" Sorry Noah, you can't ride in the front seat until you're 8 years old, it's the law in New Jersey. You have to ride in your special seat in the back."

He responds to me again as if I didn't say anything so I repeat it the same way, and then try a different approach.

" Mommy will get in trouble from the police if I let you sit in the front seat. We will not go anywhere if you are not in your special seat."

He was still not getting it but has switched gears.

" I am mad, no hitting, no scratching." He says

I recognize this as part of his social story, but not the scratching part so I make an assumption.

" Did Sami scratch you?" I ask

" No I can't go, Target's closed! Can we go to Target now?" he said immediately contradicting himself, which he frequently does.

" Just calm down, sit in your seat and we can go"

" No! Targets closed!! "He yells very red in the face "Okay we won't go." I say calmly but am starting not to feel that way.

" No I have to, can we go to Target now?"

He still insists it is closed and he can't go, but he has to go and this goes on and on for the remainder of the hour.

Eventually he just stops, gets in his seat, and says we can go to target and get gas. I don't remember ever saying we had to get gas, so he must have merged another experience from another tape in his head.

Later that night this same scenario happens again when I am getting him in the bath. We have two bathrooms-ours that is painted green, and Noah's that is painted purple. The purple bathroom is decorated in monkeys, and normally he is fine with taking his bath in there. Sometimes he likes to use ours since we have Jacuzzi jets in our bathtub, but on this night our bath is in need of a cleaning so it isn't going to happen.

"NO I need to take a GREEN BATH! " He yells

" No you can take a monkey bath or go to bed with no bath." I tell him

" Can I take a green bath? " He asks again

" No." I tell him again

" I have to! He yells, can I take a green bath?" he repeats for who knows how many times now.

" No you can take a monkey bath or you go to bed with no bath." I say as plainly as possible

He agrees to the monkey bath then as we are getting in there, he immediately changes his mind and wants a green bath, because you know he HAS TO. At this point I am not messing around and now Joe comes in to see what is going on. We undress him and just put him in the shower. After some initial screaming he calms down and is back to normal as if nothing ever happened. The shower diffuses the problem; oh if only take along showers were a plausible thing.

One part of Autism / PDD etc. is most of these kids perseverate over objects or repeat the same sequence of video over and over. Playing with toys or objects in this manner is no big deal, but when it they can't let go of something, an idea, to find an object, a horrible feeling it can be very frustrating. The feeling of needing to sit in the corner and bang my own head against the wall has made sense at times. It's not a problem when it's just the video or television program that is getting replayed over and over 57 times. Noah seems to enjoy whether it's either funny or calming you would have to ask him. But it in its normal sense is not a negative thing for the child. It may seem odd or annoying at times to the rest of us. So perseverating is not a bad thing all the time, just when it happens right before you're going somewhere or when it shows up unexpectedly in times of anxiety. When it is channeled for a purpose, it becomes being focused. So at least when getting stuck on a videotape or what have you, they are practicing this skill in a non-threatening way.

Reason indicates that if someone has a problem with obsession, you should be showing him or her alternatives to obsessing, or you need to let them just obsess. By training them to not let go because you are forcing your will, it only reinforces them to do this back to others. After all, that's what modeling is all about; we know children learn from watching us. Autistic kids have trouble learning this way naturally, which is why they need therapy. Hence, using therapy to teach modeling behavior is a double-edged sword, since there is going to be both the task at hand to learn as well as the reaction to it.

Ideally, when the child is upset over not completing the task, maybe the approach should be to listen to them and let it go for now, and bring it back later when they are not upset about it. Since most of the time, it is NEVER the object, or task, it's what is going on inside. The only way to teach them respect is to give it to them. How or why would they respect you or feel good about themselves if every time they get scared or threatened they are made to continue on as if they are not. I think that would make a person feel like they are from another planet.

This brings me to the next problem: why are we trying to bring these kids into our world without going into theirs? Do we really believe we have it right? With all of the problems people have with themselves I think maybe we should look at it another way. I personally go into Noah's world on a daily basis if possible, Frankly it makes us closer together; I don't really care what other people think about it either. I have answered the door with a trashcan on my head because that was what Noah was doing that morning. I am secure enough in myself not to worry about what I look like. I would rather know what my child is really feeling and thinking. Sometimes when he replays that same sequence over and over I can really see what is so funny about it.

Little Squares with Colors

One of the most fun aspects of having a child with an ASD is all of the fun games you get to play, such as "Where's the Poop?, Guess that Liquid! and the Autistic version of Password where you have clues and have to guess what it is he is actually upset about.

I say I need to write a Noah - English dictionary, for the sounds he makes and the terms he says that refer to other things. Perhaps by the time I complete this book I will add an appendix to start this process, if I didn't, well, I am sure you can find one reason or another throughout this book that explains why.

Noah has been in therapy for about a year and has nearly doubled his vocabulary from where it was when I was working with him, so he has about 150-200 words.
One day when Dianna is here working with him, Noah suddenly starts asking for something that is unintelligible except the words "squares" and "colors"; he gets more frustrated with us not knowing what he wants and speaks more rapidly, making it even harder to understand. The cycle of frustration, crying and the meltdown begins.

This goes on for thirty minutes, with us only understanding little squares with colors. Is it paint? Some electronic toy, something one of the other therapists had here yesterday? Something from the past that seems like it is from yesterday?
Dianna and I are wracking our brains and can't figure it out. We call others and ultimately think it's the paint with little square papers. This is acceptable to Noah and he does this, where no other redirection worked previously. So we accept this as the answer, puzzled over why he didn't just ask for paint.

Later this day, Noah asks for little squares with colors again - turns out it wasn't paint. Uh oh, looks like the paint was just an acceptable redirect, but not actually what he was talking about. Now it's going on naptime so I ask him to look in his room, since he is still calm about it.

The password is Rubik's Cube...

A few minutes later he starts gleefully yelling "I FOUND IT." I go see, and there it is - a Rubik's Cube, little squares with colors.
As in many areas of life it's the simplest answer and we just had to find it.

Autism is truly more of a test for yourself - how to think on your feet, stay calm, be patient, and apply compassion and tolerance. Maybe these kids can teach us about ourselves. Because truthfully, being able to withdraw into yourself and tune it all out is a gift and a skill, not a handicap. Only with its interference in your life is it a problem. And I am not talking about how that affects other people, as I said we need to take a lesson. If stimming helps them regulate and feel better it's really an adaptation to something the brain is not providing. If you take it away, won't that make it worse?

Obsession (between love and madness it lies) can be a good thing when channeled correctly. It helps solve problems, it helps create new inventions and it pushes us forward when we may want to stop, but are very close to the resolution. I allow Noah to obsess over the computer because he has now learned more about the computer than some adults. I let him obsess over numbers, and he has great math skills (he was working with negative numbers when he was 5) I let him obsess over the water in the bath - it relaxes him, and keeps him clean. Plus I love a good long shower, Rene' Descartes, Einstein and many other great philosophers and minds have used long baths for reflection and to solve problems. Worked well for them.

The true challenge is helping the child not feel threatened, feel safe, and when it is an obsession that is causing them to be upset, to find a way to redirect that energy. Get their mind off of what is upsetting them, not stay there. It is easier said than done much of the time, however my sister has always been a champ at this. At any given moment she can just yell, " Look, an elephant" or something similar and it always works.

I am all for teaching Noah the skills needed to calm himself and redirect himself when he is overwhelmed or full of anxiety so he knows how to fix it. I also know that his meter for calming himself is broken, so it needs to be repaired. He is limited on how he can do that for himself, but I believe he will eventually make improvements on it. I am interested to hear what new way they would like to teach that, since the last two years of theories did not work. Noah is now being taught how to maintain his stress level by being in a relaxed setting as often as possible, and by doing relaxing techniques.

Someone with a broken leg receives physical therapy to begin walking on it again after it is healed. If it happened too soon this would not heal it, they are taught to walk again after it is healed. I see his problem with anxiety just this way. A behavior plan would have to be for behaviors that are not a result of anxiety, since the symptom of that anxiety is a behavior.

Another analogy (since I love them), you have a runny nose from allergies or a cold. The symptom is the runny nose, what do you do? Don't you blow your nose for starters? Perhaps take in extra liquids, vitamins, or medication? You treat the symptom by curing the problem. If a child has behaviors from anxiety you have to make them calm to treat the anxiety, then the behavior is not relevant, just like your runny nose. Typical behaviors are different and are handled in the house, as they would be for any child.

Double session Tuesday, Noah has Dianna in the morning then Sydney comes in the afternoon; occasionally they overlap with each other. I love the meeting of the minds.

" I was thinking about instituting something called the ALERT system." Sydney mentions one afternoon

"Do explain."

" Basically we separate how his body feels and what is going on sensory wise into three categories, relating it to an engine. If he is feeling anxious, angry, or feels hyper he is over-stimulated and we would say his engine is running high. If he is feeling sick or tired, he is under-stimulated and we say it is running low. And of course when all things are just right, we call it.." Sydney said

" Just right, that's handy." I say

" We can cut out pictures of Tigger bouncing and similar cartoon friends running around to represent the HIGH, and pictures of Eeyore or Piglet looking sad or tired to be the LOW and mount them on a poster board with the words"

" Ooo, this is an excellent idea since he is so visual." Dianna says excitedly

" I used this before with another student and it really worked well, I can make him a little car or truck with a removable sticker that he can change to say how his engine is doing. This way he can have it for his teachers."

That Sydney, so brilliant. She always comes up with something I hadn't thought of, and that is not an easy thing to do since I think a hell of a lot. One day there will be a statue of shaving cream and bubbles erected in her honor.

Dianna is now leaving, and Noah is yelling out the window "Watch out! Be careful" I can hear the trash truck is coming down our street Nice, he is actually concerned about someone else besides himself.

As I am writing this Noah just comes up to me and asks "can I see *Moon Sand*" which he is referring to another document in the computer about a day he had a meltdown about the moon sand colors being mixed up. I know he means the word on the page and not the objects. How or why he remembers and associates this computer program with the time he read the words moon sand is one of those things that amaze me.

Later that fall Dianna goes back to school to finish her doctorate, and though we are happy for her, we did not realize her departure from the team actually marks the beginning of the end.

The Fall of Minding Manners

Dianna brings a sense of organization; she is reliable provided the office informs her where she is supposed to be. But best of all she gets it, she is great with Noah and we share similar philosophies on how to work with him. She just has the actual training, and her style is different than mine. I actually find her less strict and, as I said, more like a grandma, just not as old as one usually is. When we find out she is leaving we are really disappointed.

Her departure in September 2007, means she has spent just over a year working with Noah. This marked a new era with Minding Manners and with Noah, one with a parade of an unusual amount of Behavior therapists from the company. I haven't expected to also lose also another one of the therapists Noah has bonded with, and that they would be training people with Noah.

This leaves Paige, who is a great therapist, but not reliable. She is late more days than not, and calls out more frequently then all of the others combined. At first I don't hold the callouts against her, since things do come up, and I am aware of her own adult ADD. I just assume the office itself should have a replacement available. But more often they will just cancel it and bank the hours. This happened so many times, there is always about 40-50 hours available they had to use for holidays and when school is closed. To this day they owe Noah 57 hours.

This of course affects his progress and behavior; he has made such progress but it seems to have plateaued off. It's happened very gradually and unnoticed, much like the way humidity can creep up on you. Sure, you notice the air is a little heavy and you go about your day until it gets to the point where you're just relaxing in a chair and sweating from sitting. Prompting you to turn on the AC (if you're fortunate enough to have it). Noah's behavior is like this, there is such a decrease in it that it's slow rise isn't noticed until you realize how tired you are so many days in a row,

But still the laundry is not done, the dishes are piling into the sink, the gardening continues to be neglected.
Why am I so tired then? Surely it isn't because I am out having any fun.

Little Squares with Colors

One typical morning after they had been working with Noah for about a year, I get Noah and the house ready for therapy. They are scheduled to be here at 9:30 so Noah has enough time to wake up and regulate before beginning his work. I also need some time after waking to get my body moving and my brain processing. If I just jump up out of bed I am dropping things, putting milk in the cupboard and cereal in the fridge, and having trouble finding the right words when I am speaking. So I understand Noah's need for regulation, figuring whatever he is experiencing has to be ten times as bad as mine.

Noah flops himself in the chair to watch some Sponge Bob, while I get him his cereal, milk and fruit snacks.

" Paige will be here around 9:30-9:45 to play with you." I remind him. Giving Noah a countdown or letting him know when things are going to happen greatly helps his anxiety. I was more of a fly-by-the-seat-of-your-pants kind of person, so ridged structure is not good for me, it actually works against my ability to get things done. But I have no problem with keeping to a loose schedule, and that seems to work best for him. Allowing for certain activities to take longer than expected, or to shorten other ones is less stressful.

Time passes and at 9:50 no Paige; Noah is no longer in the Sponge Bob trance and is now looking out the window for his playmate.

I call the office to see what is going on, and more importantly, to update Noah. He has already asked me four times when she is coming, and I am not sure what to say anymore.

" Hi, this is Noah's mom, we are expecting Paige to be here around 9:30 and she isn't, and hasn't called, do you know if something came up or do you have a way of reaching her?"

"Oh, no one called you?" the voice on the other end of the phone asks

"Nobody has called about anything." I tell her

" Oh, sorry, we couldn't get coverage, Paige had to go help her dad today. Sorry no one called." She says before hanging up

Great, I think, well at least we aren't tied to the house now; Noah doesn't have any other sessions until 2:30 when Sydney comes over for OT. So I originally take it as good news, but am later reminded by him that it isn't.

" Sorry buddy, No Paige today. Something came up." I tell him, not expecting him to understand all of it.

He starts beeping and making noises to himself and running around. After a while when I attempt to direct him into playing the Sponge Bob Life board game I am met with the Autism monster. The Autism monster often just shows up unexpectedly, like a little switch flips on and there he is, yelling, screaming, throwing things, slamming doors and talking nonsense.

I don't notice it coming either, we each take one turn, and then he is just staring at the game board and said, " Play game"

" We are playing the game." I say to him

" No anything!" he suddenly yells

" Whoa, ok Noah, how about we go to our room to calm down for a minute" I suggest since he just went from 0 to crazy in two seconds.

" There's bugs in there." He says nervously, however there are no bugs in there. " Play game?" he asks right after

" Okay, if you calm down we can play the game." I say

" No ANYTHING!" he yells even louder fists clenched

I start walking him over to his room, which is ten to fifteen feet away from where we are playing.

" What does a cow say?" he asks out of nowhere. Then he yells " GO TO ROOM" and runs off in his room crying. He doesn't stay in there, but is back in less than a minute and yells " NO CLOSE DOOR" then is mumbling " "Tomorrow", and "Saturday", for some reason. Obviously none of this makes sense, and this is not my first experience with this monster either. No matter how many times it happens, it still is bewildering when you're in it. Because first of all, it comes out of nothing, and secondly there is so much talking that is not connected to anything you are saying.

He carries on like this for a good hour, on and off crying and babbling words that had nothing to do with anything. Eventually I put him in front of the TV and found some of his numbers and he calms down like nothing ever happened. But the day was now shot for leaving the house; since that is always a source of anxiety he has to work through. And since the water was already boiling in the pot, it didn't seem wise to turn the heat up anymore. I share my feelings with Sydney when she arrives here. Sydney now has become not just Noah's OT but part therapist to me.

" I just don't get it. How can they not have a back-up plan? This is not the first time this has happened; in fact the first three months someone was out once a week. I had to complain about it and then they seemed to try harder. Now it's been a little while so, they must have cycled Noah to the back of the line again. These are behavior experts, they KNOW how important routine is, and they demand it. They KNOW how changes in it disrupt the delicate balance."

I go on for about fifteen or twenty minutes about this subject, and Sydney is sympatric but doesn't work for them so it isn't as if she can do anything about it.

What I really don't get is that Sydney has worked with Noah by herself for as long as they have and only missed a session when she got married or had to cancel because she was sick a handful of times. The week she got married there was a replacement, and when she was sick she rescheduled while she was calling out. But it could not have been more than five times. But these people have called out at least 40 or 50 times at this point.

I have to get over it of course, can't hold onto things. And when I tell the school what is going on, they just tell me to call them when this happens again. Yay, more phone calls!

So in the fall of 2008 Dianna and Kristen are out, and in walks Keith, Meghan, Jenny, Erin, Danielle, and Jesse. Jesse was originally hired as Noah's shadow in pre-school for this school year to replace Paige who started out doing it. For some reason they never did divulge she is banned by one of the teachers there. (Probably because she is late a lot, but I am just guessing). The unfortunate part is Jesse begins her job as his shadow and has never met him, unlike Paige who has many years' experience under her belt, and late or not, knew Noah very well. She could read him, anticipate him and knew how to motivate him. Likely the problems that began in the classroom this year started with this first changing of the guard.

Jesse like many of the new people is a college student about to graduate. Not that I have a problem with that, but then I begin to realize why they are using these people with Noah. It seems like they are using Noah as a child to train with because of how smart he is, how fast he picks up things, and how dedicated and plugged in I am to his needs and progress. He has come a long way from where he started so his functioning level is much higher now that he has been receiving therapy for almost 2 years. The actual work given by the therapist is therefore more rewarding for them because Noah is able to reinforce the good work they are doing, since he is learning.

A lot of Autistic kids can take longer than Noah to learn some of the new objects or cards they are teaching, which may be a more discouraging proposition to new therapists, especially those that are unsure whether they want to do this as a career or is unsure about themselves and their worth. I get that as an approach - perhaps they figure this gets more people in a very needed field. But it is contrary to what I believe. If you want to learn how to parallel park, then practice in a van, everything else is much easier after that. Noah is not a van in the autism world when it comes to learning, he would be more like a four door sedan.
However, his ability to learn is largely due to all of the therapy we've already given him and how we lucked out by determining the right combination of foods to remove

from his diet. Dairy can be removed from every Childs diet and it doesn't even mean it would change anything if the dairy isn't affecting anything to begin with. But it could be eggs, it could be soy, it could be dyes or preservatives, or any combination of these things. The gut and brain contain a lot of the same material, and where there is a problem with one, you will find a problem with the other. This is medical fact. This for me was easy to accept after living through this and then one day going over a long list of people I know that also have "issues".

My sister and my oldest friend both self-limit their diets and certain foods do not agree with them. My sister is lactose intolerant and Dyslexic as is my friend Roxanne. Another friend has Crohn's disease and OCD; another cannot eat chicken and has other digestive issues and is ADD and has a diagnosed anxiety disorder. The list goes on. Getting control of Noah's diet is half the battle, if you can control the thing that is influencing what the brain can and can't do, you can then get control of the brain to teach what it missed out on.

I feel they should have been using these people to be filling in for when the regular therapist is out. Why not have them earn the right to be a full-time therapist, to see if they are truly dedicated or not? I know for a fact that may have kept one of them off the case, who tells me she isn't really sure if this is what she wants to do. And frankly she is such a dry person; being with children does not seem to be her forte. Regardless, they need to have back up because everyone gets sick sometimes, their cars break down, people die, but normally you don't like knowing they are choosing Atlantic City over working with your child. At least make it an international location or somewhere hard to get to.

One night in July of 2008 I am over my sister's helping her clean and pack for her move when Paige called me.

" Hi, I'm in Atlantic City and were going to stay over-night so I am not going to be there tomorrow."

Someone from this company has said this to me about 70 times at this point in the past two years, no exaggeration. Not to mention it was after 9 pm, I am not home, and even if I was Noah was asleep with the idea he has Paige coming over tomorrow. I can feel the heat of the tension rising in me as I ask the next question.

"But someone else is coming, right? "

"Uh, I don't know, I can call and find out."

I suggest she do so, because at this point I am so annoyed that I am ready to just go all mortal combat on anyone and everyone. My sister gives me a puzzled and mildly concerned look, and to ease the tension, comments about what an idiot her husband is. Or perhaps she had hopes I would direct my hostility his way. This is when I start to get angry more often, when before I was always a pretty laid back kind of person.

I think this is the last straw, but I am wrong, the real last straw is later in the month at our clinic meeting when we find out the consultant whom we had the whole time is no longer on Noah's case either. Add this to the pile of twelve. Seems they are trying to organize themselves by school districts, so now Noah has all new therapists, one super unreliable one that would rather be in Atlantic City, and a brand new consultant that has never met Noah, and is also relatively new to being a consultant.

I take some time to reflect on how I feel about the necessity of this behavior therapy. I have my questions about it, and due to the fact that the complexion of the team has changed so drastically, what at first was really helpful for Noah, is no longer working. His increasing behaviors seem to be caused by the inconsistency they have brought. And quite possibly the behavior modification plan, has not been properly modified to his own growth. So when we sit down to our IEP this summer, I have a good idea which direction I am now interested in heading.

You don't know me, you don't wear my Shoes

We walk into the conference room at the school after being directed to the wrong location at the high school, but (with a sigh), whatever.

The room is filled as usual with the same faces and some new ones: The person in charge of the study team; Noah's case worker; the psychiatrist; learning consultant; Sydney; the current preschool teacher; Becky and the new consultant of Minding Manners; and the proposed kindergarten teacher, whom I don't know but seems like a lovely woman.

" Why don't we start with Miss Sydney's report?" Noah's caseworker suggest.

" First of all," Sydney begins "I want to state there have been some very good improvements this year with him being more alert and engaged. We have had numerous difficulties in the classroom setting and worked throughout the year to make it better. I administered a Sensory profile that was filled out by Christine and Miss

Jen; Noah overall scored as a definite difference which is 2% or less of the population, indicating Noah's ability to modulate his sensory system is different than most children."

" We have been utilizing movement breaks in the classroom such as dancing, hand washing, and sitting on an air cushion. We also began the alert system this year so he could let his teachers know when he was over or under stimulated."

Everyone else goes through his or her reports, all very similar. Noah is bright, but he has trouble staying on task and being focused. He also cannot sit still for the duration of circle time. Which we found out was almost 45 minutes, and, ASD or not, what four year old can sit still for that long? Even though Noah at this time has just turned six, he is developmentally at the three-four year old level. The pre-k teacher means well, but it turns out this was her first year teaching it, and formerly was teaching high school.

He still does not socialize much with the other kids, preferring to play alone. He often talks to himself (or self-talking as they like to call it). So now when I think about Helen ,the former bag lady of our town, I realize she was really just a self-talker with an ASD. Paints a different picture now, rather than some crazy cat lady talking to herself and throwing cats at people.

" We know this was an overall difficult year for Noah , the head of the Department states, "and he couldn't finish the year, so we want to be sure we will have the right placement for him next year."

He drones on also about how many absentees Noah had, as if that is something that can be avoided. Sure for the sake of appearances. I will send him to school sick so he can wind up infecting other kids or wind up in the hospital.

I have written a detailed report for this meeting, explaining Noah's strengths and weakness and what we could do to work with them. It's our in depth analysis so there will not be much to question.

" Though we appreciate the time you put into this letter, it's a bit overwhelming." States the head of the department

I think gee, that's probably how Noah feels most of the time so I understood what they meant, and it was a lot of information, but I listened to them anyway.

" Well " I reply "with all the problems this year, and since he hates school now to the point he won't go and I had to end it, it stands to reason we need to find something that is more appropriate. If thirteen kids are too many, then a smaller setting such as his doctor recommended would be better. And since he is so bright, he needs more challenging work; he is way advanced on all the preschool work."

"We don't want to see too many splinter skills; we like to build an education from the bottom up." States one of the numerous heads at the table

"I can understand a well-rounded education, but that is what is looked at for typical kids, not kids like Noah." I question

" Your looking for a half day program, with a small group of kids that is more academic? I just think what you're looking for doesn't exist" Our caseworker said. I am not sure if she even knew what she was saying.

" There are no small classrooms of five or six kids that are for higher functioning ASD kids anywhere around here? I know kindergarten is now full day but if he is having an issue with the half-day program already then sending him full day seems, well stupid " I asked, because what they are proposing just seems ridiculous

" Children are entitled to a full day of kindergarten, other districts have to send their kids here if the parents request it."
"So there are half-day programs, why can't Noah go to one of them?" Joe chimes in

"It's the timing of it, since they have caps, we may not be able to get him in, but I don't know of any classroom that is this small or has just an Autism class."

"Well, then I guess there needs to be one." I say flatly

What is most annoying about these conversations is we had a meeting about it four months ago, knowing that, with him going into kindergarten and having some issues this year, we would have to find the right class. Joe and I sat down with Noah's caseworker for over an hour going over these exact same issues.

"Really it doesn't exist," Becky nervously laughs

"Well, neither did school until someone made one, neither did any of us until our parents made us. I don't see how that matters." I antagonize. People hate it when I am logical; it crumbles their whole argument most of the time.

They go on and explain how the class they picked for him was wonderful; yeah it had twenty kids in it, but the teacher is great. And she looks pretty sad during this meeting as if the problem was her personally, and just from meeting her I felt she would be a great teacher for Noah. If only she could have him for half the day and with half the kids. They do not seem to want to address anything we were asking about, and are ignoring the fact we already discussed these possible problems 4 months before.

We leave the meeting feeling frustrated, because still nothing is resolved. What I don't understand at all is what do they think will happen when Noah is sent into a more difficult setting than he already experienced and grew to hate. Kids of five or six shouldn't hate school, for if they hate it now, what will they think of it later when they get a lot of homework, and it's more work than fun?

By August I still haven't received the IEP in the mail, I am also disenchanted with Minding Manners. If they can't get their logistical skills down, why not have the college kids or interns be floaters? What is so difficult about this idea? Or having any ideas?

The first day of school comes and goes but I don't know it since I never got a calendar; I only knew when it was because I ran into an old friend at in town who told me about her kids going to school. So I figure, I will wait and give them rope. They made this mess, so they can clean it up. I clean up enough messes I do not create. For once, I decided to let someone else handle it.

They call me after noticing Noah was not in school.

" What class?" I ask them. "We never received the IEP, I never received notice of which classroom he would be in, or even what time school starts. So even if we were going to try a new situation, we don't know what it is."

That weekend I put the paper on my desk and a sign from above is visible

Maple Shade Nursery and Kindergarten, full and half day. It was right on Main Street in our town, across the street from my sister's house. Couldn't be any more convenient, I called them after looking at the website, liking what I see so far.

" How many kids are in the class?' I ask

" There are five children enrolled." The woman on the other end of the line answers

Wait a second, this is a kindergarten class, with 5 kids, in Maple Shade and you have a half day program. The kids work with computers, and it's mostly academic. Yes Virginia there is a Santa Claus, look at that, it does exist! I think to myself

" You can bring him in and see for yourself."

I went over there the next day with Noah. The building is an older stone house, that I have seen in our town my whole life. It has a friendly, but secluded feeling. The drive way is lined with big wooded drawings of his favorite Pooh characters. The windows also display similar artwork. The back of the building holds a bunch of playground equipment, slides, things to climb on, and swings. Perfect. We later dub this place Pooh and Piglet Corner, to make it sound friendly and not use the word *School* since he pairs that word with much unpleasantness.

Noah takes off right away and starts touching sand, climbing things and talking to himself, (excuse me, Self-talking), as he always does. I have already informed them he has issues but told them if they were fine with a shadow, then he would be fine. He just needs someone to help explain things he still doesn't understand verbally and to keep him on task.

The price is very reasonable-about $400 for the month, nothing to school district, and it wouldn't need to be for the whole year, just long enough to reprogram him to think school is cool.

So we sit down again for yet another meeting, and Noah's caseworker is excited about this place. They organize an in-service to explain Autism and its cousins to the people of Pooh & Piglet Corner. The new consultant is to go over there as well, but couldn't make it, but fortunately Noah's former was able to do it.

All of this is handled in about a six-week period at the beginning of the 2008-2009 school year. When we sit down yet again for another IEP meeting and have to listen to this new consultant from Minding Manners who had met Noah maybe for twenty minutes two different times, trying to sound like she knows anything, I just lost it, and fired them. She may be the expert on her own children, but, with all of the grief they have put us through, finest group of people or not, they were not helping Noah make any meaningful progress anymore. Their usefulness has run its course, like a dial on an old television set.

The next road bump (or glitch as his caseworker put it), is that the county doesn't want to pay for it. So I decide I will pay for it then, and will work it out with the county later. The law is free and appropriate education for all children, not free OR appropriate. But this is what they say, that I can have a free education for him in the public school which isn't appropriate because of the class size and time in the classroom. Or we can have an appropriate education for him, but we will have to pay for it.

The school should then have to provide a shadow from the educational services unit, the dreaded unit that Minding Manners frowned upon. However, they sent a very smart and lovely girl, who worked great with Noah for three whole days before the county, citing the No Child Left Behind law, refused to pay for it, because the teacher wasn't accredited. Before this law all teachers who taught kindergarten were certified to do so based on holding the appropriate degree. And considering she had taught kindergarten there for 20 years, this made her qualified, until the law changed requiring teaches to have additional certification based on subject and level. Regardless, kindergarten is voluntary, and the County may have been in the wrong, it is not going to get Noah in school any faster by taking them to court.

So now we have no shadow, so I do what anyone would do. Go to people I know that know and love Noah and work with kids.

Nick has always worked with kids, or plants actually. He has held jobs at Disney World, a YMCA, and a Boy Scout camp every summer most of his life.
He is also an Eagle Scout, and most importantly Noah worships him. Nick stands over six feet tall and his height just amazes Noah who comes from a family of short people.

By this point Noah has missed the first month of school, went three days and now I have to get Nick fingerprinted again, even though he had it done three times already. Gee I love New Jersey and its pointless laws that only generate more paperwork and justification of jobs that are meaningless, but that is a different book.

So onto Grandma, since it was going to be a month for them to process Nick's paperwork, Grandma drove a school bus for many years and had worked in a day care center recently. She is also now retired, and is his Grandma; it was fine to keep him in line for only two months. I just want him in school and to get to the Christmas break at this point.

Noah loves Pooh & Piglet corner, I have no problems getting him to go - I was right about it being a better setting. But he does need a teacher more suited for him, and a professional shadow.

" I am sorry this isn't working," they say to me one November morning after Noah has been there almost a month. " He is too distracting to the other kids"

" So he's not welcome here," I ask

" No it's not that he's not welcome, I just thing he needs a professional shadow."

" Well then I will get one." I tell them

" I just don't think this will work"

" I don't understand. We sat down about this in the fall and now it's not working? You were told what to expect, and you know my situation. I have appreciated any help you have given but now you're saying he's not welcome?"

They don't have a more satisfactory answer, and at this point I am tired of people's words that don't mean anything, or mean something else. Suddenly I can appreciate these kids not wanting to talk - look at the world they're in.

I take Noah out of there and never look back. By December he is ready to try the public setting, and since he now likes school again we were over that hurdle. The school is also now willing to not enforce the full day that he of course was entitled to, this set of compromises and outside-of-the-box thinking is what got Noah to be successful in kindergarten. I also give them credit for matching him with wonderful kindergarten teachers who understand and appreciate Noah for all he is and all he isn't.

Now we will be continuing on with OT and speech therapy, Noah will also have a shadow to help him stay on task and to bring him out of the room when he needs a break. He has increased his vocabulary to that of a kindergartener and his behaviors are as under control as they can be without medication, there is no need for behavior therapy. We still implement a token system for good behavior and he loses them for bad behavior, so he will have to earn them back to gain his reward. I have no regrets on these decisions; they were the best choices for Noah. The behavior therapy did provide a much needed foundation, and it ran its course.

ACT THREE

Pieces of the Puzzle

A School Writing Assignment

Noah had to fill in the answers to the following questions; you will notice a common theme.
FYI- At the time his computer was broken by him and he has been without it for about 2 month.

The best thing about me is: **Weather**

My best school subject is: **Computers**
Because: **I like computers**.

When I am home I like to: **Play on the computer**

I am happy when: **I go on computers**

I get mad sometimes because: **I never get mad** (this is just a lie)

When I am sad I like to: **take a break**

Once I was scared when: **I see my first grade teacher**.

When I am in 6th grade I hope: **there are computers there**

When I am in high school, I would like to: ***go on the computers***.

When I am 25 I hope I will be: ***A weather man.***

If I could have 3 wishes for my future I would wish: ***To be 30 yrs. old, weather man, and No Mondays.***

"Build me an Ark Noah."

This is one of my dad's longest running jokes regarding Noah's name. On any day where it has been raining for what feels like 40 days, I look around checking to see if Noah is indeed building an Ark. He is known to take apart most of his toys and reassemble them to be other things. Even stacking toys, board games and books to represent other items, usually the pieces are parts of a video game that exists in his mind. One morning near the end of the school year, I find him in his playroom sleeping under the computer desk, the environment surrounding him in disarray. Small bins from the toy box lined up along a wall, board games stacked on their sides in piles as tall as him. And finally the chair from the desk that is in his bedroom is in the middle of it all. Noah has trouble falling and staying asleep-most nights I have to police the house until he is out. But I too need my rest, so sometimes he is still awake when I pass out. This is such a night; I wake him up to get ready for school and when I ask him if he had a party out here. He says no, apparently this was his house, and the board games were his TV. (Suddenly the chair makes sense.) "What is this pile then" I say, pointing to the next pile on the side of the "TV"

"Oh that's my stereo, and this is my Wii" he proudly says; showing me his Dr. Seuss board game next to it.

He goes over to the last pile and tells me that is his stove.

"But Noah you have a play kitchen right there, it has a stove."

"But this is a big one."

Well, can't argue with that kind of logic. We agree that if he is going to do this he has to put the games away before school if I am cleaning in there that day. So, today with the constant rain, I figure I would check, just in case he is building an Ark, because with him you never know. I just hope those nasty robins are not the privileged few to get on the Ark.

Noah suddenly announces "We should catch that crazy robin"
There are two, possibly mental challenged robins wreaking havoc on my car and driveway this past week. I have never seen birds act like this, and probably could easily say all of the bird poop that has been put on my car and driveway in the past week would equal the amount I have seen on all my cars for the past seventeen years. These birds land and dance on the car, they peck at it, they try to bite it, flying with their mouths open as if they are going to swallow the car whole. They of course also poop all over everything, causing me to clean the car four or more times a day unless I want my paint to come

off. The dancing robin was cute at first - even Noah had an impersonation of it, hoping around singing " dun da dun da dun da.."

"So you think we need Pop pop to get those birds?" I ask Noah in the car on the way to school after he was talking about needing my dad to catch them.

"Yeah, we should put him in a cage, feed him and fly him around." Noah says

Pop pop, would not likely wish to feed or water these birds, or fly them around. Not after all this aggravation, and Pop pop's desire to eradicate pests that try to destroy his habitats or possessions. Of course this is the same man that swears he hates cats, but has been spotted spoon-feeding some sick kittens. Overall I was grateful Noah even made these statements, it is nicer than what he said first.

"We should kill him!"

I am not sure what Noah actually understands about death, or killing. He seems to think to kill is just to "knock out" There have been numerous times I have tried to explain to him what he may be thinking about is not the same as what I or whomever else he is with at the time is also thinking. He often requests for us to pick an activity, but what he really thinks is we will pick what he is thinking. And when we don't he gets very frustrated and ultimately upset. Trying to explain death or murder is hard to explain to a typical child, let alone one that has the universe only exist in their own mind. Its Noah's world and we are just living in it.

What is truly important about the comments on the birds was he was actually thinking about it on the spot and expressing it. Statements like this have not come naturally for a very long time, so when one pops up, it is a small victory. Parents of typical children rejoice and feel delight over their child's accomplishments as they occur, for parents of children with Developmental delays, these occasions do not happen in those early years, but they do happen. Our rejoicing moments are just delayed, which in turn makes them all the sweeter.

The rain has become a source of concern and wonder for Noah. He has been obsessed with weather, checking it on the computer or the Wii multiple times a day. Most people think he will be a meteorologist one day. And until recently, it was never a source of anxiety, just obsession. One day while picking him up from school in the middle of a sudden torrential downpour, a huge thunderclap came overhead, and since then he has been living in fear of thunderstorms. Now if it is raining, or the weather alludes to the possibility of a thunder shower, he is nervous, unable to sleep and keeps coming out of his room, saying he cannot sleep in there, asking numerous times to check the computer. He generally walks around with a blanket over himself, much like Linus and his blanket. There have been times where I found him in his bathroom at a time he and I should have been sleeping, with a portable DVD player, and his furry friends all camped out in there since there are no windows in that bathroom.

Fear of thunderstorms is a typical fear for most children at least at some point in their lives. But for Noah, it is not easily comforted. Despite getting him several books on weather and reading them with him, despite explaining what is lightning, both what it is, and the kid version. ("It's just the clouds taking pictures like your camera".) Despite telling him thunder is just sound, and he can think of it as Pooh and Tigger bowling and they just got a strike, he is still extremely worried and scared. Worried that the house is going to catch on fire, and who knows what else that he can't verbalize.

Each time there is a storm though we have to start over, as if we didn't already take any steps, or had any conversations regarding the thunder and lightning. This is both frustrating and exhausting for all involved. How I long being able to go to sleep at a normal hour. Even tonight, I return from my sister's house to find him asleep on the kitchen floor, blankets over his head, and weather station next to it so he knows the time, and his two Webkinz Jr pals. I carry him to his room and fortunately he does not wake up. But I have to wonder what happened and why was he there? I am pretty certain that by the morning he will not know.

Santa Wishes.

It's Thanksgiving 2008; Noah is gaining more language and probably has the longest conversation with us ever, possibly even to this day. It starts with overhearing him talk about having a mouse and cutting a hole in the wall.
"I should need a mouse, talk". Noah stutters out to Joe
"But mouses don't talk."
"Some mouses". Noah questioningly insists.
"Pretend Mouses". Joe gently jokes.

Noah skips off into the other room to work on his computer. My sister and I are in the kitchen and are now intrigued. So I ask
"So you want a real mouse, but cut a hole in the wall? Like Jerry." I assume he means from Tom & Jerry, he loves those cartoons.

"Yeah, like Jerry" Noah says while working on his computer dragging out the yeah.

"I thought you meant a plush toy, you mean a real mouse"
"Yeaaahhh and a plush toy. How about both. A plush toy and a real mouse. "Noah says without even looking at us, but hard at work on something.

"Well you'll have to ask Santa." I say because I am not sure what else to say here.

"Will Santa bring a real mouse?" Noah asks

"Well I don't know if he can bring live animals overseas." I scramble with. I can't believe he is still talking about this, and I am so amazed and enjoying it, my mind cannot come up with much else. He suddenly gets up and pops his head into the kitchen.

"Or mom, I can knock on the mouse's home and he comes out every time! So I knock and he comes out and I'll hold his hand. And I can sleep with him. I think maybe he must have his own bed."

We are laughing pretty hard at this point because of how much thought is going into it. Noah seems pleased, we encourage him to keep coming up with new ideas by prompting him with "and what else would he have"

"Oh well I think he must have his own telephone and his own *fridgerator*." He also adds "A TV and maybe a DVR and a VCR."

"Ooo and we can have a picnic too. He can call every friend, every mouse, every time." Noah adds, being sure to drag out the word time.

"He can knock at the door and I can let em in."

"Oh we aren't going to have lots of mice in the house." I say semi-sternly because, no.

Discarding what I just said Noah adds
"Oh yes how about every mouse at the mouse's store"

Then he asks my sister "Do you have a mouse?"
"Well not since we moved" she says.
"Well where is the mouse?"
"We left it at the old place." She says with laughter.
"Well someone has a mouse." Noah says to the floor, almost disappointed.

"You know your mommy use to have pet rats." She says, just pushing the subject more. Noah is not as enthusiastic about rats.

"Pet rats. Nooooooo. I don't think pet rats, I don't think" he says and then goes on to explain. "Pet rats are wild. But mouses are fine. Cause mouses are nice!"

Noah did get a plush Jerry. But no mice. He forgot about this conversation thankfully and never brought it up again. If he lived with my sister however, it would be a different story. She was ready to go out and buy a dozen after this.

"And the dreams that you dare to dream really do come true."

Plush, soft furry little friends all lying about the playroom floor, just waiting to be picked up. Waiting to be taken to a nice place where they will be loved, licked and possibly chewed on a bit. This is how Fred sees Noah's stuffed animals, and also what I think he is thinking when I see him and Sami at a standoff. Sami must be one big moving stuffed animal to Fred, and all he wants to do is pick him up in his mouth, lay down with him and lick him.

Sami on the other hand has no interest in this activity whatsoever. He will swat and growl at Fred like he always does, and eventually they move to separate other corners. What I find amazing is how new this seems to Fred every day, even though all three of them have been living together for two and half years. But to Fred it's like the first time, every time.

Fred walks around with the same sock in his mouth, his tail wagging, all in the hopes that Sami would want to play tug of war with the sock. He approaches Sami, tail wagging faster, grin on his mouth getting bigger, and he starts to curve himself toward Sami as if to say "Come play with me." Sami responds with one of his meows that indicates he is not interested.

"He just keeps trying, no matter how many times Sami rejects him." I think realizing how wonderful that part of his personality is for helping Noah also. No matter how moody Noah is, Fred always wants to play with his little buddy.

The sock game is one of his favorite games to do with me when I finally lie on the couch at the end of the day. I've taught Noah how to play this with Fred but he still prefers just running and having Fred chase him.

Chewie is not one for the sock game; he does not generally seem interested in wanting to play the same as Fred, who will bring you the sock or another toy if he wants you to play with him. Noah most of the time prefers to play with Fred because Chewie jumps a lot more and "doesn't listen" as well.

It is the first day of summer vacation for Noah in 2009, and the first day of triple time for me. It already starts off great with him not getting asleep until almost 1 am last night taking me longer to get to bed myself. So, when he comes bursting in my room this morning yelling through a giant wrapping paper cardboard roll, to make it all the more loud. I know I have arrived.

I sit up and can hear the tapping sounds of the dog's nails on the hard wood floor of the living room. Judging from the noise, both dogs and boy must be involved in some activity. This is enough fear to get me to sit up and get out of bed before my body was ready. I know I will pay for this later by being extra clumsy and having great difficulty with most fine motor tasks until my brain catches up with my body.

Noah and the dogs are just running around playing hide and seek. They do this sometimes, he will get ahead of them and go hide behind Joe's big over-sized "dad chair". Chewie and Fred will then promptly go find him there, because it's the only place he hides. Dogs have happy grins on their faces, tails are wagging and there is laughter from Noah. Okay, no crisis, good maybe; I can make some coffee to wake up fully.

"Get it Chewie!" Noah yells at the dog, which is jumping up gracefully to grab a partially deflated balloon leftover from Noah's Birthday. "Look he likes it!" Noah laughs in glee as Chewie proudly trots off with the balloon in his mouth. Fred is standing there watching it all with a big smile on his face.

Noah retrieves the balloon and repeats the same sequence - he throws it up in the air, and Chewie catches and again trots away. And I have to mention how much this normally awkward and sometimes skittish dog is moving so gracefully like a show horse.

I have seen him do this before with Noah and Pillows, for whatever reason he loses his awkwardness if he is carrying something in his mouth Noah has given him. I get out my camera to take some photos and video of this big fun moment of boy and dogs running and chasing balloons but it is about to be cut short.

" I smell poop." Noah notifies me

Sure enough there is a lovely pile on the floor in the playroom, obviously fresh. I look at the clock and discover it is almost ten; I normally let them out between seven-thirty and nine o'clock. So I immediately start to take them outside when Noah asks me "Can I take a picture of the poop?"

" No that's disgusting."

" I will do it." Noah says, not understanding that I don't want that as a picture. As I am letting them out I now wonder if he is in there taking pictures of the poop. Well, it's a digital camera, I can always delete them, I figure as I then go clean up the mess.

Noah did not photo the poop, thankfully.

"Noah you were right I should have taken them out, I didn't realize what time it was. I wonder which one of them did it?"

" Chewie did it." Noah says knowingly

" How do you know that is was Chewie?" I asked

"That's the color of his poop."

Well, okay then, didn't realize there was a difference in the color of the poops, but if there is, Noah would notice that. I laugh to myself, glad that Noah did have a reason that he was able to pull out of his brain like that. That hardly ever happens.

For the record, when the dogs did go out, only Fred went number two.

Fred is soon to be taking the AKC Good Citizen test so he can later compete in trials and for his therapy dog work. I can have him certified to work without it, but if he were to do any of therapy for other people it would benefit him to have it. The test is not that long and contains about ten basic dogs skills. The first three tests have to do with him sitting politely for petting and grooming and allowing strangers to speak to me without him getting aggressive. These will be okay once I can get him to stop wanting to jump on people and lick them to death. Even dogs appearances are judged in this world, and fortunately for Fred he is a very beautiful dog.

The next two tests are to take a short walk on a loose lead and walk through a crowd of three people politely, this we will have to work on. I know he is fine on a leash, but it's the polite part I will have to verify. The final parts have to do with responding to "sit" and "down" commands and to come when called (which we have down) and reaction to distraction. This is where I know Chewie is not ready; for he is distracted by distractions, go figure. Fred can stay focused if we are walking through the room and people are walking around throwing crutches and wheel chairs. As long as I have a cookie in my hand, I am confident he will also be confident.

The final certification will be the proverbial icing on the cake. The true reason we got the dog (well now dogs) was to help Noah with anxiety and bring him out of himself, to help him relate to another living thing. And these furry heroes have done this; they have helped reach Noah in their own way and are more tolerant and patient than any human that has interacted with Noah has been. They have been useful in helping us manage ourselves with their unconditional and boundless love - it's hard to stay upset when you have two adorable dogs smiling and wagging their tails at you in anticipation of giving you kisses.

They have also learned to alert me when Noah is up and about at night, and can even go to him on command by being told to "Go get Noah." Off they run through the house to find Noah which is normally followed by squeals of glee and laughter and some nights when they all pass out together in Noah's room, Autism or not, all is right with the world.

"You're Gabby's Laptop." A Glance into the mind of the Literal Thinker.

One of the more amusing sides of Autism is how the mind of the person takes all things literally. So if you say it is raining cats and dogs, well the child really thinks there are dogs and cats coming out of the sky. At least Noah did; once when I said this, he kept staring out the window and saying. " I don't see it, where are the dogs?"

Another time is when Chewie had been misbehaving for excessively jumping and I put him in the Florida room while Noah, Fred and myself still played outside.

" Where's Chewie?" Noah asks

" Sorry Noah, he was bad for jumping. So he can't play with us right now. I am a little mad at him so he's in the dog house." I try explaining.
Noah runs around the yard asking "Where is it, I don't see it?"

" Don't see what, buddy?"

" The dog house."

I have explained what a figure of speech is, but it seems to go in one ear and out the other. So I find it amusing most of the time. When I get a song stuck in my head Noah wants to see it, and now he offers to help rinse it out. Now that he has more language he can expand this a bit. Saying that it's a disc in my head and we need water.

I first notice the literal thinking, when I teach him to wash his own hair.

" Ok, now you have the shampoo on your head, so put your hands on your head"

Noah does this while standing in the shower.
"Okay, now move your arms back and forth."

He drops his arms to his side and swings them back and forth. After this I am more careful when explaining things, than I already was. I am especially concerned with explaining what would happen if he got shampoo in his eyes. I think it's best to leave the burning part out, because I have the image of him seeing flames shooting from his eyes. And if he thought that, he would never use shampoo again.

I still have to watch the figures of speech; I really am surprised how many there are: Daddy's on a roll! I am so hungry I could eat a horse!

Sometimes it's best to not say anything.

But it's not only those fun little statements we sometimes say. He has truly tried to learn how to tell jokes and even comes up with his own comebacks. For a while he would just repeat whatever I said back to me. If I tell him he was being a brat, he told me I was. If I said you're going to go into time out, he tells me to go to my room for time out. After this goes on for about a week one day his comeback takes the cake...hahaha

Noah is working at my computer while my sister and his cousin Gabby are visiting. Gabby had brought with her this pink Disney princess laptop she had received as a gift, and even though it was for girls, it was still a laptop and therefore was something for Noah to covet. He multi-tasks with it and the real computer. Gabby wants it back though, so my sister asks about it.

"Ok Noah, I want to give Gabby back her laptop." Jenn says to him

" You're Gabby's Laptop." Noah replies with conviction

" Well...okay " Jenn laughs "Can't argue with that." Which is a miracle. This is a person who can argue with anyone over anything, and should be a lawyer. It is amazing there is someone who can come up with an argument she can't participate in.

For whatever reason, for weeks after this, whenever Noah wants to be silly and call names this is what we have to call him. He calls me a toaster or a stove, and I have to call him Gabby's laptop. At least this time I know the answer. For $1000.00, this is something you are, "What is Gabby's Laptop." See, everything as Jeopardy makes sense.

Now of course there are those other words in our language that people never really understand but accept. Questions we have heard at some point in life like, "why do you drive on a parkway but park in a driveway", or "why is a Brillo pad called Steel wool", when it isn't steel or wool. These are the types of words that to Noah and other kids like him that paint confusing pictures. These words we take for granted, because we all accept it, and hardly no one really questions them.

" Mom, my head is hot." Noah says but not really looking sick

" Your forehead is a little warm." I respond fluffing his hair.

" I don't call it my forehead, I call it my one head." He replies, trigging a memory of him asking me why it was called a forehead. Which at the time I didn't have much of an answer for. I remember then him saying it was just one head. I must have been tired and didn't get it.

The literal thinking though explains a lot of the communication problems. If Noah makes pictures in his mind based on what we say, anytime something that doesn't match the picture there are problems. Now I understand why telling him to go to the door when we get out of the car yields better results than to go into the house, because I didn't say to open the door and go into the house, just go into the house, which may be a confusing idea since we cannot walk through walls.

He also refers to his "running nose" as a walking nose.

"I will walk around and it will be better." Noah said regarding his runny nose

I learn that I just really need to listen to what he is literally saying so when he asks, "What happened before the marker broke", even though the marker isn't broken, he is not delusional - he wants to know what CAN happen to make the marker or whatever item he is talking about break.

This aspect of his personality combined with the fact he still struggles with many concepts is where there can be big communication problems. The trick is finding that balance of talking about things in enough detail, but not over talking since too much talking drives him crazy. At least we all know he thinks with pictures. All we have to do is remember that when talking to him.

So why is it that the latest news is the most current news, but if your late for an appointment you're not on time?

Noah's Letter to Santa Claus as dictated to me Christmas 2008

Dear Santa,

I would like a thermostat in my bedroom and I need an elevator in my bedroom too! And another TV so I can have 2 VCR's in my bedroom. Oh and don't forget the intercom and fire drill. How about a nice quiet fire drill so it makes quiet sounds.

How are you doing? In case you can't bring that stuff I would like a Tigger & Roo and Buster and Darby on Scooters. And a rescue pet swimming in the waterdog, and that's it!

Oh yes and a Pink Panther Plush and Lights for Daddy.

Your best pal
Noah
and Fred and Chewie the dogs

Fear and Loathing in Autism

Yesterday, Noah was incorrigible, and very mean, as he can sometimes be. He more often is not mean as much as he just doesn't get it. But it was one of those days where he is behaving like someone who belongs in an institution and that will create a feeling of longing in me to send myself to one.

"Shut up, I'm going to kill you!" Noah yells at me while also throwing everything he can find in my general direction.

"That is not okay Noah, now you need to go sit in your room for a few minutes and cool down." I say very firmly, on the verge of anger.

"I don't care, I don't like you!" He screams and is running from me now.
"Now you are turning a minor thing into a big thing, all I wanted was to see what you are looking at on the computer."

I go to turn off the computer and take him to his room when he smacks me with the plush toy in his hand. I try to reason with him, all he had to do was show me what he was looking at, and he went from zero to crazy in seconds. But hitting is not tolerated, nor is speaking to me that way. This is the third anxiety episode of the day; the others were over trying to make cookies. I figured I should leave him be for a while when it wasn't going positively, so working on the computer is normally a good activity for him. But like all parents I monitor what he is doing on there. Normally he doesn't care, but for some reason my presence upset him, it was the first time he was so violent in a long time.

It takes some time but I eventually get him into his room after being hit repeatedly, and screamed at.

Accompanying this type of day with already not feeling well created a feeling of not caring. I didn't care about finishing this book, or writing any book. All I could see was curling up in bed and just lying there. However, in the back of my mind a voice said, *you know this is temporary and later you will be just fine*. Which was true, I wasn't turning cartwheels later, but did feel better, and by the next morning I was back to normal, back to writing this book. Those moments happen to us, even when we logically know better.

People often can't help themselves when it comes to looking into the future. Especially parents - there is so much to pay attention to when raising children and so it's natural to have concerns. Sometimes people will often try to look into that crystal ball to see what is ahead for their child, and when your child has any kind of developmental or even medical problem you may not have always been looking for the best outcome. You may be looking at the things you fear.

Unfortunately if you get stuck there, the results will be as you envisioned or at least close to it. This happens with other parts of our lives as well, having a tendency as humans to worry more than necessary and creating those things we fear. People will make decisions based on their attitude and sometimes it's helpful, like taking vitamins or locking your car so no one steals it. But if you go too far and take a lot of vitamins, and add a lot of different products to your body because you fear of being ill, you may wind up so because of all the different products. Same goes for taking locking your car to an extreme, if you wrapped your car up in chains and all sorts of do dads, wouldn't that draw attention to it? A would-be thief might now notice your car, whereas before it was just another one in the lot.

There is a lot of talk about thoughts being a tangible energy, and this is why the rich stay rich and the poor stay poor in most cases, because they are fixated on where they are. I don't know how much truth is in that or not, the jury is still out. But I do believe we make subconscious and even conscious decisions that affect our lives and propel us forward or backward based on how we feel. This is why some people sabotage themselves; it seems crazy that someone would not want things to be better. Success can be scary because it's so close to failure. What would you do once you succeed? Maybe, the real test is not worrying about it. But again, easier said than done, just like most things it takes practice.

Each day is a new chance to do better, be better, work harder, and get closer to that which you want to become. Frankly if you didn't believe things could be better than you would have never read this or any book about Autism. So, inside us, we do believe things can be better, it's our nature to have goals and improve, otherwise we would all be living in caves and no one would have bothered inventing the wheel.

Sometimes I forget about all that we had to do to get to where we are now with Noah. It can happen easily when you have adapted to your life and things become normal, even if they aren't normal things for other people. I forget about the 30 hours of therapy here a week doing Behavioral therapy, ABA, speech and OT, the endless parade of people and their toys in and out. I forget how it took until he was five and half to get him potty trained, that it was through years of trying, plus one intense month of living in the bathroom. I forget about the fact I still shop at three to four different stores to get the right food, the never ending search for better and new OT toys, the fact there are bottles of bubbles in every room in this house, bottles of lotion, flashy things, spinners. I forget that nearly all of our credit card debt is really therapy debt, since there is only so much help available.

Sometime I forget about how we rarely go anywhere, and nearly never out with friends. I forget to call my friends because there is always more work to be done, and when there isn't and the house is quiet, I need quiet more than I need companionship, since my life is very full with communication, even if it is mostly one-sided.

I forget because it's been years and it has become the norm, and I don't remember what it was like before now, I forget because he has made such improvements. He no longer spins himself and walks on his tippy toes, and rarely flaps his hands, He rarely ever bangs his head, though he does still hit it and himself when frustrated. My dad says he does that because it feels so good when he stops. The meltdowns that used to be an hour or more long sometimes several times a day have decreased in time and how often. I forget because now he is talking even if it isn't the same as other 7-year-old kids; he is talking and telling jokes, and saying things like *you're Gabby's laptop*, but also saying things like *you're the best mom ever*.

He is giving hugs where before he did not want to be held, he is more understanding of what he shouldn't be doing, he corrects himself more and apologizes more on his own. He actually wants friends now and was so sad the other night when he couldn't play with his new friend Elise from his class. He was even upset one day when she was in time out and couldn't join the class in whatever activity they were about to do. Noah actually sat there and cried, but Elise didn't really care she was in time out. She probably was grateful for it. Of course the next day he popped Gabby in the face for taking his robot's remote control, and though it's never ok, for a person to hit another person, it is typical of young kids to do that. Noah may be physically seven and should be past this phase, but he is mentally not there yet. Baby steps. It doesn't mean he won't get there; it just may not be on the timetable we would have expected.

But we have come a long way.

From Dogs to Autism

I wake up today thinking about evolution after watching *I Am Legend*. For some reason, what grabbed me most in that movie was the relationship between Will Smith's character and his dog. It made me think about how having dogs and cats as pets is really nature's little miracle. They are animals and they share their love and devotion to us; sure it has a lot to do with the fact we care for them and feed them, but it wasn't always that way.

I am thinking about Charles Darwin and how his theory of evolution has a lot to do with adaptability and gene mutation. I figure that it also has a lot to do with how an animal's brain adapts to its environment. Domesticated dogs are not trying to eat us as food because they have been trained over time with a person providing it for them, so that part of their brain for survival is suppressed. It's not missing, rather other parts have grown because of the stimulation they receive from their "owners". I begin to think how this relates to humans.

The theory has a lot to do with Man evolving from a more primitive brain to what we have now. Figuring at some point, Man was more Ape or Chimpanzee like. Human and chimp DNA is very close and only different by a few markers. Darwin was right about his natural selection; I just think there is more to it, because of the time involved in the process.

This leads me too Autism and how Joe always says it's the next evolution, and I think he is on to something. It is the breeding that messed me up with this thinking. Because we always think of evolution as breeding, those traits are passed down, and they come from a gene mutation. That part is true, but there is also another element. The element of how the brain adapts just like the domesticated animals did. So it's not just that children with Autism are the ones evolving, the people who care for them and their brains are evolving as well.

One thing we do know is that the brain is very malleable and has much plasticity; it can change from where neurons are firing and where they are not. Our brains at one time were much more fixated on survival (reptilian brain) but the other parts have always been there, just not used. It is a scientific fact we do not use all of our brain at the same time. Perhaps it is a necessary part in the chain of evolution.

Perhaps Autism is more of an evolutionary journey and change. With the world becoming more computer driven and less things done by humans, the idea that we would be less social and more fixated on numbers is the way it is, so maybe DNA changes, mutates to accommodate. Maybe it's supposed to be this way and we are trying to fit people to be what we think they should be. Maybe that's not our job to change it all, in the sense of making Autism just go away completely to make the people who have it just like the rest of us. Maybe what we are supposed to be focusing on is to help, guide and love. Help balance them, guide them in life, and love them no matter how they act or whether you feel love back. This is something I want to continue to chew on.

As far as behaviors, in a lot of cases it really reflects the viewer not the doer. Just like many things we have opinions on what is right or wrong, often reflects the person with the opinion more than the person who has the "problem."

Many people have been guilty of seeing a mother or father out in public somewhere with their "unruly children," assuming they must be poor disciplinarians allowing their children to walk all over them. How can anyone know that just from seeing these complete strangers in a store? By making that statement, you are assuming that because your children, or pets or children-to-be will not act this way, because you are or will be a good disciplinarian. It falls into that same category of where people put other people down to feel better about themselves. For if someone else is a creep, you must not be; if someone else dresses poorly it's based on how you must not dress as bad as them. If you had known that those kids had a sensory disorder and to them all the noise was like being at a construction site, and the lights were so bright it felt like their eyes were burning, you may understand how they may not be in the best of moods, for you wouldn't be either.

How much I have learned. There was a time when I cared or had concern with what other people thought of my parenting skills. Now I know how much I have taught him, how much I will continue to teach him, and how much he has taught me. I have spent more of my life not really worrying about what other people think. But I didn't fully actualize that until Noah, I didn't fully get why I felt that way. Now I know what my dad really means when he says "opinions are like assholes, everyone has one and they all stink." My opinions are my own, and not everyone will agree with them, and that is fine, that is what makes the world go around. And just like people will not agree with me, I will not always agree with them.

Listening to what your own inner voice says is what matters most, not what someone is saying behind your back and not to your face; not what someone says that does not know the full situation, not what someone thinks when they may be jealous.

Considering my main philosophy of life is to have balance, and Autism is mainly a disorder of imbalance, getting Noah balanced will be the actualization of my own life. This is why it all makes sense to me, having a naturally balanced child would be no challenge at all.

Sympathy for the Autism Devil

Night time is a problem more so since the school year started. At least he is willing to go this year, which is not the way it was last year. And his behavior after school is better, though still exhausting. But by night time he is still really wound up; he has a regular bed time routine and despite that and plenty of activity, and all of the other things we are doing, he can't seem to settle down any earlier than 11pm. It is really frustrating and exhausting for us, because there is no time to ourselves. He will come out and interrupt us, and I have to wait up until he is asleep no matter how tired I am. Thankfully the melatonin has helped with this. Otherwise he will be up until the wee hours of the morning, which has happened a few times when my body simply gave into the sweetness of sleep.

Unfortunately no matter how Zen like a person is, when you're sleep deprived and have no time at all to yourself except the seven hours you are asleep, and in my case it's like sleeping next to a running lawn mower, your ability to be creative and patient is greatly diminished. So when

Little Squares with Colors

Noah is having a horrible time getting to sleep, so are we and everyone can wind up crying.

Tonight he is bouncing around so much in his room, I can hear all these crashing sounds of him throwing himself off the bed onto the floor. I go in to find out what was going on.

" How is your engine? Is it too high or too low?" I ask him

" It's freaking out." he replies. So Joe gives him some squishes and crashes and it helps a little, but it is a shame because Noah truly wants to sleep to and is crying about it also. After he calms down some, and is lying in his bed I read him *Go Dog Go* and say my goodnights.

"Good night buddy, you get to sleep in late tomorrow. No school and nothing to do." I say as cheerfully as possible

" Oh I have things to do tomorrow, I have to take care of my pets, play brain challenge and get my brain up."

"Oh you're right you do need to log into Webkinz and Webkinz Jr. Are all your pets okay?" I ask

" Time is not okay, he is hungry, bored and tired, but his health is fine."

I begin to search the radio because the station he listens to that normally broadcasts jazz, was playing some mambo, (or samba I can never tell the difference) music tonight. There are no other stations playing classical or anything remotely relaxing but the church channel, that plays choir-type music and people reading scriptures.

" I don't like that channel" he says when I stop on the church channel.

I flip around some more and go back to the mambo / samba station.

" No No, I don't want quiet music, try again," he insisted sleepily

" Oh, you don't want quiet, then what kind of music do you want?"

" Cool music." He answers. I flip around the stations some more, landing on a classic rock station playing "Sympathy For the Devil."

" Here you go Noah, it doesn't get much cooler than The Rolling Stones."

The radio sings "Please to meet you, won't you guess my name, and what's puzzling you is the nature of the game."

I close the door to his room and ponder the meaning of the song, how in some ways Autism is the Devil, and also how you can have sympathy for it, that it is misunderstood but still holds a purpose. Good often triumphs evil, because part of being good is the fact you can understand evil's place, but evil doesn't get the value of good. But what rang loudest was how Autism is often referred to as a puzzle, and indeed this was the nature of the game. Many people have sadly felt that Autism was the end of their dreams, and for them I hope they change their minds so they don't miss out on the fact that it isn't the end, it's the beginning of dreams you didn't know you had.

Overall Noah is getting better every day thanks to changing his diet, understanding his sensory needs and thinking outside the box. Life with Noah is more of a test of tolerance and patience. For with all he throws at me, I have to adjust, dig deeper, and think further outside the box, all of which makes me better for it. For that I thank him.

I still try to balance the amount of help to give. When learning to ride a bicycle, we learn often from falling. Anyone with a mental or physical issue will fall more often, is it our job to clean them up and care for them after they fall, or is it our job to prevent them from falling so much? Considering there is only so much falling that is teaching anything. Maybe it is both, and because there is that much more work for those of us who care for them; this is why we should take better care of ourselves.

I am not going to pretend I have all the answers.

And on this day and this evening of tucking him in Noah is here, very present, much like any other child. Tomorrow may be different, I won't know until tomorrow happens.

When he is here, and with us it is like being in a green park or on a beach with the sun shining and the breeze just right. The type of moment where, whether you believe heaven is a physical place or not, you know you are having a glimpse of it. All the worries you have, don't matter, and what it all means, doesn't matter either.

It's good to have him with us, even if it is just for the day.

Epilogue

This is not a book about finding a cure, it is about acceptance and in the time that has passed since I wrote the final words of the final chapter Noah has improved and still has many issues. It is anyone's guess how impaired he would be today if not for early intervention, if not for the many things we have done. If not for persistence, if not for luck. But most importantly if not for the crazy belief things could be better.

We have since taken our very first family vacation to Disney World. It in itself was a huge feat, not just the financial challenge, but for taking Noah out of his comfort zone, his need for structure, and the obvious challenge of all the stimulation, people and dietary needs Disney is extremely accommodating about these things, they have dietary options for all kinds of people, they offer a mobility pass for anyone who can't stand in long lines (you get in a shorter one, or a time to come back), Overall they wanted to make sure we could have as good of a trip as anyone else, and just thinking of that brings tears to my eyes, since much of the world really doesn't' care how hard things are for you, to just be as well off as them.

Little Squares with Colors

We have previously had struggles just going out to eat, sitting in a movie, playing mini-golf and fishing. This was a huge deal because of being so far away from home for many nights. It took a lot of preparation and planning. Would the car ride be too much, it was going to take two days, would we be insane by the end? We weren't sure if this was going to be worth it, but when you spend most of your time not being able to have any fun, and it's been almost a decade since you have been anywhere awesome, you might be willing to try.

The car ride wasn't as bad as it could have been. However I do not wish to see or hear any Clifford the Big Red Dog episodes for a very long time. Noah was comfortable in the back seat of our sedan with his favorite blanket, a boat load of "friends" and a portable DVD player. I am reasonably certain all kids need to go the bathroom often, so besides that it was easy. We arrived at night in Orlando; we head to the Kingdom the next day.

We have a group with us on this trip that consists of my Dad, Ginger, Gabby, Joe's Mom and friends of ours and their two kids. We are staying off property at a timeshare about 5 miles from the gate of Magic Kingdom, in what is known as the "Downtown Disney" area.

The next morning we headed out. It was a beautiful day, sunny and warm but not hot, very nice for December. Noah and Gabby were holding hands excitedly on the tram that leaves the Magic Kingdom parking lot and takes you to the monorail or boat. Even getting into this place is an adventure.

"You're the best Noah ever!" Gabby shouted to Noah

"You're the best Gabby ever." Noah replied back to Gabby as the tram rumbled closer to the park entrance.

It really is a magic kingdom I thought to myself, and was then overcome with emotion. We had arrived, we were approaching the gate, after two days in the car, and years of preparation, after all the practicing, learning, the sacrifices, after even nearly not being able to be here, we made it, and we were here! Tears welled up in my eyes over how grateful I felt, finally on vacation, we made it.

Disney wasn't so magical that there were no melt-downs; there were probably four the first day, one within twenty minutes of this moment. And there were still many to follow, plus we did spend quite a bit of time at pay phones, one of Noah's fascinations. But all and all it was way more successful than we had hoped. I hope the next time we return it will be a bit less work, but never-the-less, even with the work, it was still a wonderful time that would have never happened a few years before.

It was 6 days of magic for certain. It encouraged us to try for more fun; just turns out we needed to be in the right place. Somewhere he wanted to be, somewhere that was willing to make it work for us.

~~

A few weeks ago while watching a few minutes of *American Idol*, I noticed a contestant that seemed to rub the judges the wrong way. They didn't like his attitude, which he had plainly stated if he had one it was because of the waiting. What I noticed from there was how judgmental and mean one of the judges was about this honest comment. Based on his "social skills" and the fact he didn't get what they were saying I would bet he is on the spectrum somewhere, and the truth is, waiting is very hard for them. I was discussing this one night with Sydney where I discovered we both felt the same way about that moment on the show, even though we were watching it in different houses. She brilliantly put "Well you and I see the world through some Autism-tinted glasses" and I think she is right, and for that I am grateful.

Why this has happened wasn't important - what we learned from this experience is what mattered. Autism teaches us to be more tolerant, more patient and never to give up hope.